Charis Bible C

CHARIS
HEALING
UNIVERSITY

Section 2
EXPERIENCE:
How to Receive Healing

Charis Healing University
Section 2: EXPERIENCE: How to Receive Healing

ISBN: 978-1-59548-427-7

Published by Andrew Wommack Ministries, Inc
Woodland Park, CO 80863
awmi.net

Printed in the United States of America.

Table of Contents

How to Use Your Charis Healing University Curriculum

Whether you are teaching a class, leading a small group, discipling an individual, or studying on your own, this curriculum is designed for you! Here's how it works:

Curriculum Components:

Each lesson consists of a **Video Outline**, **Lesson Review Questions and Answers**, **Points to Ponder**, **Go Deeper**, and **Scriptures** section. The **Go Deeper** section includes **Self-Examination Questions**, **Prayer Points**, and **Action Steps**.

Outline for GROUP Study:

I.   Group leaders can prepare for each session by:

    A. Printing a copy of the curriculum components for each member of the group

    B. Reviewing the previous **Video Outline**

II.   Begin each session by watching the **Video Lesson** as a group, and follow along with the **Video Outline**.

III.   Read each **Lesson Review Question** aloud.

    A. Discuss possible answers.

    B. Encourage everyone to participate.

IV.   Read the **Lesson Review Answers**.

V.   Review and discuss the **Points to Ponder**.

    A. Each point may be read aloud by the group leader.

    B. Group members may take turns reading the points aloud.

    C. The group may read the points individually and share thoughts at the end.

VI.   Individually review the **Self-Examination Questions**.

VII.   Select a group member to create a prayer using the **Prayer Points**.

VIII. Read the **Action Steps** aloud to the group.

IX. Individually complete the **Action Steps** in your Healing University journals.

X. Encourage the group to meditate on the provided **Scriptures** throughout the following week.

Materials Needed:

Charis Healing University book (or print-outs), Bibles, writing utensils, and journals (dedicated to Healing University) for each group member.

Outline for INDIVIDUAL Study:

I. Begin each session by watching the **Video Lesson**, and follow along with the **Video Outline**.

II. Read each **Lesson Review Question**, and consider your own response.

III. Read the **Lesson Review Answers**.

IV. Review the **Points to Ponder**.

V. Ask yourself the **Self-Examination Questions**.

VI. Create a prayer using the **Prayer Points**.

VII. Read and complete the **Action Steps** in your Healing University journal.

VIII. Meditate on the provided **Scriptures** throughout the following week.

Materials Needed:

Charis Healing University book (or print-outs), Bible, writing utensils, and a journal (dedicated to Healing University).

Lesson 1
Why Are We Sick?

Instructor:
Andrew Wommack

VIDEO OUTLINE

Note: All scriptures used in this lesson are quoted from the *King James Version*.

I.   Some causes of sickness are just natural, and other times they have a spiritual root. It is helpful to discern why we get sick and where these sicknesses come from.

A. Not everyone wants to be made whole.

> *And a certain man was there, which had an infirmity thirty and eight years. When Jesus saw him lie, and knew that he had been now a long time in that case, he saith unto him, Wilt thou be made whole?*
>
> John 5:5–6, *KJV*

B. Jesus told him to do something that he couldn't do.

> *The impotent man answered him, Sir, I have no man, when the water is troubled, to put me into the pool: but while I am coming, another steppeth down before me. Jesus saith unto him, Rise, take up thy bed, and walk.*
>
> John 5:7–8, *KJV*

C. You need to start pushing yourself and doing something that you don't feel like doing.

> *But wilt thou know, O vain man, that faith without works is dead?*
>
> James 2:20, *KJV*

II. Sin is an inroad of sickness into your life.

> *Afterward Jesus findeth him in the temple, and said unto him, Behold, thou art made whole: sin no more, lest a worse thing come unto thee.*
>
> John 5:14, *KJV*

A. Sin opens the door to Satan who comes to steal, to kill, and to destroy. He will do it through finances, emotions, broken relationships, and also sickness.

The thief cometh not, but for to steal, and to kill, and to destroy: I am come that they might have life, and that they might have it more abundantly.

John 10:10, *KJV*

B. If you have lived in sin, you have opened up a door to the devil, and you need to shut that door. You need to rebuke the devil, command him to get out, and then lock the door.

C. If a person is living in sin, and if sin is the avenue that Satan has into their life to bring sickness, God still loves them and wants them well. But you're actually doing them a disservice to just minister healing to them without confronting the sin. They will go back and live in that sin, reopen the door, and then that sickness will come back seven times worse.

D. God's healing comes by grace, but there are consequences to sin.

Know ye not, that to whom ye yield yourselves servants to obey, his servants ye are to whom ye obey; whether of sin unto death, or of obedience unto righteousness?

Romans 6:16, *KJV*

E. All of us sin by just failing to be the perfect person that we should be. There is a difference between a sin of omission, where you just aren't the perfect person that you know you should be, and a sin of rebellion, where you are absolutely persisting in something, yet you're asking for all of God's benefits while you're serving the devil.

F. God loves you, but you are giving direct inroad to the devil, and God gave you authority over the devil.

Submit yourselves therefore to God. Resist the devil, and he will flee from you.

James 4:7, *KJV*

III. There are some sicknesses that are just natural.

A. God gave you wisdom to use your faith and believe, but at the same time, there are some things that are just natural.

B. When you start experiencing some natural pain, you ought to recognize that there are some things that are natural and quit doing what causes you pain.

C. If you're doing something in the natural that is causing you problems, then there needs to be a natural response, although it can be coupled with a spiritual response.

D. If there are some natural things that are happening to you that are exposing you to sickness and disease, you need to take some precautions and deal with those things in the natural.

E. Physical accidents are an example of natural sicknesses.

F. Perhaps you have not taken care of your body. There are physical consequences of abusing your body.

G. You need a combination of saying, "God, forgive me. I draw on your power. I receive your healing," and quitting those natural things that are causing you to be sick.

IV. There are some sicknesses that are just demonic attacks. Now, some of these things overlap because Satan can't just have access to you without your consent and cooperation.

A. Suppose somebody around you caught a communicable disease and you inadvertently receive something that you didn't really want. It wasn't your sin that caused it to come. Nonetheless, there is something coming against you. It could be a demonic attack that you did not welcome. But in a sense you allowed it because you didn't stand on the promises of God's Word.

B. If we were all walking in the Word of God perfectly, I believe we could actually keep sickness from even coming nigh our dwellings.

There shall no evil befall thee, neither shall any plague come nigh thy dwelling.
Psalm 91:10, *KJV*

C. Sometimes we aren't releasing our faith the way we should, so Satan can just come and attack us.

D. Some things are not anybody's fault. Some things happen and they're demonic attacks.

E. Some sickness can be a direct demonic attack. I believe that if you are trying to heal something that is demonic in origin with some natural, organic method, it will be ineffective.

F. There are ten different times recorded in the Gospels where Jesus cast devils out of people. These people were afflicted by:

1. Blindness and not being able to speak (dumbness) – Matthew 9:32–33, Luke 11:14, and Matthew 12:22

2. Insanity, seizures, attempted suicide, foaming at the mouth, gnashing of the teeth, and screaming – Matthew 17:14–18, Mark 9:17–27, and Luke 9:37–42

3. Being bowed over (scoliosis or curvature of the spine) – Luke 13:11–13 and 16

G. Jesus healed people that were not oppressed of God but of the devil.

How God anointed Jesus of Nazareth with the Holy Ghost and with power: who went about doing good, and healing all that were oppressed of the devil; for God was with him.

Acts 10:38, *KJV*

V. Everything—all sickness, accidents, and tragedies—are somehow or another the result of this fallen world.

A. The Bible says that in heaven there won't be any sickness or disease. So we can pray for that healing and wholeness right here on earth.

Thy kingdom come, Thy will be done in earth, as it is in heaven.

Matthew 6:10, *KJV*

B. If you get the flu, yes, believe God for a healing, but at the same time, wash your hands, and quit going around people who have the flu (quit exposing yourself to it). There are some natural, common-sense things that you need to do in addition to standing in faith.

C. There are sometimes that Satan comes against you with a sickness or a disease. When it's a spiritual attack like that, you have to fight it in the spiritual realm.

D. You may be able to survive with sickness caused by the demonic, but you aren't going to have total freedom until you recognize that it is demonic.

E. Jesus commissioned His disciples to go out and heal the sick.

> *And when he had called unto him his twelve disciples, he gave them power against*
> *unclean spirits, to cast them out, and to heal all manner of sickness and all manner*
> *of disease.*
>
> Matthew 10:1, KJV

VI. You need to pray and let the Holy Spirit show you the cause of the sickness.

A. If there are things in the natural that you are doing that's causing sickness—whether it's sin, or simply doing something in the physical that's damaging your body—quit doing those things. Then believe for the supernatural power of God to flow, and you will walk free from them.

B. If it is just an attack of the devil trying to stop or hinder you from doing what God called you to do, then you must overcome it in the spiritual realm.

VII. You need to commit yourself to do what you know God has told you to do and then draw on the power of God. God will keep that which you commit to Him.

> *For the which cause I also suffer these things: nevertheless I am not ashamed: for I*
> *know whom I have believed, and am persuaded that he is able to keep that which I*
> *have committed unto him against that day.*
>
> 2 Timothy 1:12, KJV

LESSON REVIEW QUESTIONS

1. What causes sickness?

2. What are some ways to deal with the causes of sickness?

3. According to John 5:1–6, what is another reason why someone might stay sick?

4. What warning is given in John 5:14, and how does that apply to healing?

5. What are some sicknesses that were mentioned in the Bible as being caused by demons?

6. Why is it important to know the root cause of the sickness?

Want more information on Charis Bible College?

Please call **719-635-1111** for information on Charis Bible College or for prayer.

awmi.net | charisbiblecollege.org

1. What causes sickness?

   The causes of sickness can be a person opening the door through sin, thus bringing consequences; doing something naturally that causes it; and being under demonic attack.

2. What are some ways to deal with the causes of sickness?

   Possible answer: Pray and ask God to show you the cause so that you can deal with it effectively; deal with natural sicknesses by quitting the natural behaviors that cause them; deal with sin by no longer knowingly participating in that sin; deal with the demonic by casting out the demon.

3. According to John 5:1–6, what is another reason why someone might stay sick?

   A person might not want to be made well.

4. What warning is given in John 5:14, and how does that apply to healing?

   Jesus warned the man to sin no more or something worse would come upon him. If I know the cause of my sickness and keep doing it after being healed, I open the door for something worse.

5. What are some sicknesses that were mentioned in the Bible as being caused by demons?

   The Bible mentions these sicknesses caused by demons: blindness, not being able to speak (dumbness), insanity, seizures, attempted suicide, foaming at the mouth, gnashing of the teeth, and being bowed over (scoliosis).

6. Why is it important to know the root cause of the sickness?

   If I know the cause, I will know what weapons to use. If it is a natural cause, I will use natural methods; if it is caused by sin, I will stop sinning; if it is a demonic attack, I will use spiritual weapons.

POINTS TO PONDER

- As long as you can stand being sick, then you will be sick. As long as you can tolerate or live with it, you will. You need to reach a place where you say, "I'm sick and tired of being sick and tired, and I've had all of this I'm going to take."

- Satan has many ways he comes and steals from you, but one of them is through sickness. If you're living in sin, and if you recognize that you're living in sin, stop it.

- If God only healed people who were worthy, none of us would get healed.

- If you are living in sin, you are just giving Satan freedom to steal, kill, and destroy through many different avenues, and one of them is sickness.

- If you are yielding yourself to sin, you are yielding yourself to Satan, the one who authored that sin, the one who tempted you and drew you into it. You have given him the right to oppress you.

- Until you quit cooperating with the devil and giving Satan place in your life, you're going to be ineffective at getting rid of the resulting sickness. If you do get rid of the sickness and receive healing, he will be able to try and enter back in—and it'll be seven times worse—unless you've stopped the sin.

- If you know that there is something you're doing in the natural that is causing you problems, then quit doing it.

- If you are speaking forth your faith and taking your authority, I believe it can be like a force field around you that can keep evil things from coming.

- Sometimes you just weren't walking in the blessing and the defense of the Lord the way you should, so it's just a demonic attack.

- All sickness is from the devil. There was no sickness until sin entered the earth.

- Many people ignore the fact that a lot of sickness is just demonic attacks against them. They're trying to go to the doctor to find some physical way of dealing with a spiritual problem.

- God wants you to be well more than you want to be well! If you will pray and open your heart up with humility, accept if the Lord tells you that there's something you're doing wrong, and then follow His direction, you will receive from Him.

- If you're living in sin, stop it. If you're doing something in the natural that's causing these problems in your body, stop it.

- If it's a spiritual attack, you aren't going to be able to deal with it in some physical, natural way. You need to deal with it spiritually by taking your authority and fighting against it.

GO DEEPER

Self-Examination Questions

Do you really want to be healed? Have you grown accustomed to your sickness? Have you gotten to where you can live with it?

Do you think your sickness could be caused by sin, natural causes, or demonic attacks? Why? What will you do now to deal with the cause?

Prayer Points

In Section 1, a personalized prayer was written to help you pray and to learn how to pray powerfully. In Section 2, use the prayer points to write and to pray your own powerful prayer:

- Thank God for His desire for you to be well.
- Thank God for not creating sickness.
- Ask God to help you discern the cause of your sickness.
- Rebuke anything demonic in Jesus' name.
- Commit to quitting something if necessary.
- Commit to changing something if necessary.
- Commit to being vigilant to do what you know you should do to avoid sickness.

Action Steps

- In your Healing University journal, copy the following, and use it as a checklist:

  When something comes against me, I will pray and ask God:

  - Am I opening up a door to the devil?
  - Have I welcomed something in through sin?
  - Is this caused by something natural that I've done?
  - Is this a consequence of sin?
  - Have I previously lived in sin and given Satan a legal right to afflict my body through some sickness?

When I discern that my sickness is as a result of sin or other natural causes, I will come against it in the natural by:

- Stopping the sin.
- Stopping whatever I know is naturally causing it.

When I discern that my sickness is a demonic attack, I will come against it in the spiritual by:

- Casting out the demon.

- Settle in your heart that some sicknesses are the results of sin, some have natural causes, and some are demonic. You need to spiritually discern the cause of the sickness and deal with it accordingly. Stop sinning, stop doing what naturally causes it, and cast out the demons. Examine your heart and, when you are ready, make the following declaration, and don't waver from it:

I believe that sin, natural things, or demonic attacks cause sickness. I will ask God to show me what causes my sickness and deal with it.

_____ (sign and date)

- Write your own answer to this question: *Why are you sick?*

SCRIPTURES

Why Are We Sick?

John 5:1–4 (*KJV*)

After this there was a feast of the Jews; and Jesus went up to Jerusalem. Now there is at Jerusalem by the sheep market a pool, which is called in the Hebrew tongue Bethesda, having five porches. In these lay a great multitude of impotent folk, of blind, halt, withered, waiting for the moving of the water. For an angel went down at a certain season into the pool, and troubled the water: whosoever then first after the troubling of the water stepped in was made whole of whatsoever disease he had.

John 5:5–6 (*KJV*)

And a certain man was there, which had an infirmity thirty and eight years. When Jesus saw him lie, and knew that he had been now a long time in that case, he saith unto him, Wilt thou be made whole?

John 5:7–8 (*KJV*)

The impotent man answered him, Sir, I have no man, when the water is troubled, to put me into the pool: but while I am coming, another steppeth down before me. Jesus saith unto him, Rise, take up thy bed, and walk.

James 2:20 (*KJV*)

But wilt thou know, O vain man, that faith without works is dead?

John 5:9–14 (*KJV*)

And immediately the man was made whole, and took up his bed, and walked: and on the same day was the sabbath. The Jews therefore said unto him that was cured, It is the sabbath day: it is not lawful for thee to carry thy bed. He answered them, He that made me whole, the same said unto me, Take up thy bed, and walk. Then asked they him, What man is that which said unto thee, Take up thy bed, and walk? And he that was healed wist not who it was: for Jesus had conveyed himself away, a multitude being in that place. Afterward Jesus findeth him in the temple, and said unto him, Behold, thou art made whole: sin no more, lest a worse thing come unto thee.

John 10:10 (*KJV*)

The thief cometh not, but for to steal, and to kill, and to destroy: I am come that they might have life, and that they might have it more abundantly.

Matthew 12:43–45 (*KJV*)

When the unclean spirit is gone out of a man, he walketh through dry places, seeking rest, and findeth none. Then he saith, I will return into my house from whence I came out; and when he is come, he findeth it empty, swept, and garnished. Then goeth he, and taketh with himself seven other spirits more wicked than himself, and they enter in and dwell there: and the last state of that man is worse than the first. Even so shall it be also unto this wicked generation.

Luke 11:24–26 (*KJV*)

When the unclean spirit is gone out of a man, he walketh through dry places, seeking rest; and finding none, he saith, I will return unto my house whence I came out. And when he cometh, he findeth it swept and garnished. Then goeth he, and taketh to him seven other spirits more wicked than himself; and they enter in, and dwell there: and the last state of that man is worse than the first.

Romans 6:16 (*KJV*)

Know ye not, that to whom ye yield yourselves servants to obey, his servants ye are to whom ye obey; whether of sin unto death, or of obedience unto righteousness?

James 4:7 (*KJV*)

Submit yourselves therefore to God. Resist the devil, and he will flee from you.

Hebrews 12:15 (*KJV*)

Looking diligently lest any man fail of the grace of God; lest any root of bitterness springing up trouble you, and thereby many be defiled.

Ephesians 4:27 (*KJV*)

Neither give place to the devil.

Psalm 91:10 (*KJV*)

There shall no evil befall thee, neither shall any plague come nigh thy dwelling.

Psalm 91:7–8 (*KJV*)

A thousand shall fall at thy side, and ten thousand at thy right hand; but it shall not come nigh thee. Only with thine eyes shalt thou behold and see the reward of the wicked.

Psalms 91:2 (*KJV*)

I will say of the Lord, He is my refuge and my fortress: my God; in him will I trust.

John 9:1–3 (*KJV*)

And as Jesus passed by, he saw a man which was blind from his birth. And his disciples asked him, saying, Master, who did sin, this man, or his parents, that he was born blind? Jesus answered, Neither hath this man sinned, nor his parents: but that the works of God should be made manifest in him.

Mark 1:32–34 (*KJV*)

And at even, when the sun did set, they brought unto him all that were diseased, and them that were possessed with devils. And all the city was gathered together at the door. And he healed many that were sick of divers diseases, and cast out many devils; and suffered not the devils to speak, because they knew him.

Matthew 9:32–33 (*KJV*)

As they went out, behold, they brought to him a dumb man possessed with a devil. And when the devil was cast out, the dumb spake: and the multitudes marvelled, saying, It was never so seen in Israel.

Luke 11:14 (*KJV*)

And he was casting out a devil, and it was dumb. And it came to pass, when the devil was gone out, the dumb spake; and the people wondered.

Matthew 12:22 (*KJV*)

Then was brought unto him one possessed with a devil, blind, and dumb: and he healed him, insomuch that the blind and dumb both spake and saw.

Luke 13:11–13 (*KJV*)

And, behold, there was a woman which had a spirit of infirmity eighteen years, and was bowed together, and could in no wise lift up herself. And when Jesus saw her, he called her to him, and said unto her, Woman, thou art loosed from thine infirmity. And he laid his hands on her: and immediately she was made straight, and glorified God.

Luke 13:16 (*KJV*)

And ought not this woman, being a daughter of Abraham, whom Satan hath bound, lo, these eighteen years, be loosed from this bond on the sabbath day?

Acts 10:38 (*KJV*)

How God anointed Jesus of Nazareth with the Holy Ghost and with power: who went about doing good, and healing all that were oppressed of the devil; for God was with him.

Matthew 6:10 (*KJV*)

Thy kingdom come, Thy will be done in earth, as it is in heaven.

Matthew 10:1 (*KJV*)

And when he had called unto him his twelve disciples, he gave them power against unclean spirits, to cast them out, and to heal all manner of sickness and all manner of disease.

Mark 16:18 (*KJV*)

They shall take up serpents; and if they drink any deadly thing, it shall not hurt them; they shall lay hands on the sick, and they shall recover.

2 Timothy 1:12 (*KJV*)

For the which cause I also suffer these things: nevertheless I am not ashamed: for I know whom I have believed, and am persuaded that he is able to keep that which I have committed unto him against that day.

Lesson 2
The Power of Imagination
Instructor:
Andrew Wommack

Note: All scriptures used in this lesson are quoted from the *King James Version*.

I.   The Lord talked about seeing our imaginations, and the imagination of the thoughts of our hearts was evil.

> *And God saw that the wickedness of man was great in the earth, and that every imagination of the thoughts of his heart was only evil continually.*
>
> Genesis 6:5, *KJV*

A. The word "mind" is the Hebrew word *yester*, and it literally means "conception." So, the mind is where you conceive things, just like a woman conceives a child.

> *Thou wilt keep him in perfect peace, whose mind is stayed on thee: because he trusteth in thee.*
>
> Isaiah 26:3, *KJV*

B. This exact same word that was translated "mind" was translated "imagination" in other places in the Bible.

> *And the Lord came down to see the city and the tower, which the children of men builded. And the Lord said, Behold, the people is one, and they have all one language; and this they begin to do: and now nothing will be restrained from them, which they have imagined to do.*
>
> Genesis 11:5–6, *KJV*

C. You use your imagination every minute of every day. Your imagination is the part of you that conceives. You cannot do something that you can't conceive on the inside, and conception takes place in your imagination.

D. The dictionary defines imagination as your ability to see something that isn't present or real at that moment.

II. You have to see yourself healed. This is a major problem in many people not receiving their healings because those that have been sick for a long time see themselves sick; they think sick, and they plan sick.

For as he thinketh in his heart, so is he: Eat and drink, saith he to thee; but his heart is not with thee.

Proverbs 23:7, *KJV*

A. Often, we just pray for a person and then they wait to see if the pain is gone. If whatever they're praying over is gone, hallelujah, but if it's not, they just go and never seen themselves healed.

B. We would be better off to instill healing in a person's heart, then let them conceive healing and give birth to it.

C. The way most people get healed is that they run to somebody else who has spent time and has conceived healing, and in a sense, they have a surrogate birth through somebody else.

D. God has some people in the body of Christ with special gifts, and you can run to them and receive healing through them. However, you can't count on that person always being around when you need them.

III. The best way is for you to conceive healing and for you to see yourself healed.

A. The Word of God is a seed, and if you will plant it in your heart, it will eventually begin to conceive and sprout, and you will see yourself healed on the inside. Once you get healed on the inside, and you see it on the inside—it's just a matter of time until the physical realm lines up.

Being born again, not of corruptible seed, but of incorruptible, by the word of God, which liveth and abideth for ever.

1 Peter 1:23, *KJV*

B. See what the Word of God says, what it promises, and then use your imagination to see that come to pass in your life.

Art thou greater than our father Jacob, which gave us the well, and drank thereof himself, and his children, and his cattle?

John 14:12, *KJV*

C. There are a lot of people who are seeking to be healed, and yet, they've never conceived it in their imagination.

IV. Our weapons are so powerful that they can cast down imaginations.

For though we walk in the flesh, we do not war after the flesh: (For the weapons of our warfare are not carnal, but mighty through God to the pulling down of strong holds;) Casting down imaginations, and every high thing that exalteth itself against the knowledge of God, and bringing into captivity every thought to the obedience of Christ.

2 Corinthians 10:3–5, *KJV*

A. There's only one scripture reference that uses imagination in a positive way. You cannot remember anything without using your imagination.

O Lord God of Abraham, Isaac, and of Israel, our fathers, keep this for ever in the imagination of the thoughts of the heart of thy people, and prepare their heart unto thee.

1 Chronicles 29:18, *KJV*

B. Hope is about the future. It's the ability to see something that you can't see. A positive imagination is what the Bible calls hope.

For we are saved by hope: but hope that is seen is not hope: for what a man seeth, why doth he yet hope for? But if we hope for that we see not, then do we with patience wait for it.

Romans 8:24–25, *KJV*

C. When you pray, you wait for the answer in the future. It might be a short period of time or a long period of time, but it's in the future. You have to believe you've got it now, and you do that with your imagination.

Therefore I say unto you, What things soever ye desire, when ye pray, believe that ye receive them, and ye shall have them.

Mark 11:24, *KJV*

V.   Faith is the ability to see something with your heart. It starts as hope, which is your imagination seeing something that isn't yet real. Once your imagination goes to work and you start seeing what you want to come to pass, your faith will bring it into manifestation.

> *Now faith is the substance of things hoped for, the evidence of things not seen.*
>
> Hebrews 11:1, *KJV*

A.   If you haven't seen it in your heart, and if you don't have a hope of being healed, then you won't have faith for being healed.

> *For whatsoever is born of God overcometh the world: and this is the victory that overcometh the world, even our faith.*
>
> 1 John 5:4, *KJV*

B.   Some of you are praying for healing, but you don't have any hope. You may ask somebody else to pray for you, but if you go away still in your wheelchair or in pain, if nothing changes, you think, *Well, that's kind of what I expected.* So, you didn't have hope; therefore, faith didn't produce.

C.   We have underestimated the power of hope, so we've tried to skip it and go straight into faith.

D.   Your imagination works in the unseen realm. Once you see it, then you don't hope for it anymore.

VI.   Meditating on the Word is imagining. You have to take scripture, meditate on it, and think about it. Just mull it over and over until it forms an image on the inside.

A.   From your meditation, your imagination will be quickened, and that's how the Word will become alive to you.

B.   The word "seed" is *spora* in the Greek. *Spora* is a derivative of the word *sperma*, which is where we get our English word "sperm" from. The Word of God is a sperm, and if you take it and meditate on it until it forms an image on the inside of you, you will conceive healing. It may take a period of time, but you'll eventually give birth to your healing.

C. Your imagination will conceive healing, and once that happens, it's just a matter of time until the birth comes. But you can't have the birth without the conception.

VII. Nothing will be restrained to you when you can imagine it with your heart.

1. How does the Bible present imagination?

2. How does Proverbs 23:7 relate to imagination and healing?

3. Why do you think some people rely on other people's prayers for healing rather than getting a picture of their healing on the inside of them?

4. If the Word of God is a seed, what should be done with that seed to produce healing?

5. How does Mark 11:24 relate to imagination and healing?

6. Give an example of a scripture that you have meditated on until it became real to you.

Want somebody to agree with you in prayer?

Please call **719-635-1111** for prayer or for more information on Charis Bible College.

awmi.net | charisbiblecollege.org

LESSON REVIEW ANSWERS

1. How does the Bible present imagination?

   In most scriptures, imagination is referred to as negative or evil. A positive imagination is what the Bible calls hope.

2. How does Proverbs 23:7 relate to imagination and healing?

   As a man thinks in his heart, so is he. By imagining your healing, you are thinking about it, and it will manifest.

3. Why do you think some people rely on other people's prayers for healing rather than getting a picture of their healing on the inside of themselves?

   Possible answers: People are at different levels of spiritual maturity and some may have a low level of faith and need a stronger believer's prayer of faith; sometimes people are too lazy to do the work of meditating on scripture to get that picture of healing inside themselves.

4. If the Word of God is a seed, what should be done with that seed to produce healing?

   Meditate on the seed and plant it in your heart. It will conceive and sprout, and you will see yourself healed on the inside. Once you see yourself healed on the inside, it is just a matter of time until it manifests in the physical realm.

5. How does Mark 11:24 relate to imagination and healing?

   When you pray, you believe you've got the answer because of your imagination. It might be a short period of time until you see the manifestation, but it's in the future.

6. Give an example of a scripture that you have meditated on until it became real to you.

   Answers will vary.

POINTS TO PONDER

- The ability to see something with your heart, not just with your eyes, comes from your imagination, and it isn't just for children.

- A picture is worth a thousand words. If you can't picture something on the inside, or if you can't see yourself healed, then you won't be.

- If you constantly see yourself well, then that is going to reproduce itself in your experience, and you will see that healing manifest.

- If you are operating in hope, then you are looking at something that isn't present or real at this exact moment. You're looking into the future and you're seeing what can be instead of what is. This is vital when it comes to healing.

- Many people are just throwing a prayer out toward God in desperation, and if the symptoms leave, hallelujah. But they don't have any ability to see something with their hearts. They only go by what the doctor says and what their bodies feel. However, you can get to where what you see with your heart is more real to you than what you see or feel in your physical body.

- Faith gives substance, tangibility, and reality to things hoped for. What if you don't hope for anything? What if there isn't any hope? Well, then, faith has nothing to make manifest. Faith doesn't have anything to accomplish.

- Hope is what controls your faith, so before you can really believe for something, you've got to hope for it.

- You've got to develop hope, and once you turn that hope on, like a thermostat, the power unit of faith starts kicking in.

- It's good to read the Word of God, but most people don't meditate until those words paint a picture.

- One of the hardest things you'll ever do is get to where you aren't walking by sight (by what the doctor says, what your body tells you, and what other people have to say) but by faith. This is where you take the Word, the incorruptible seed of God's Word, and you meditate on it day and night. If you keep doing that, it will paint a picture on the inside of you.

- You need to have a vision for healing. You need to imagine yourself healed. Meditate on the scriptures until you can see yourself healed, and once you see it on the inside, it's just a matter of time until you see it on the outside.

- Meditate on the scriptures concerning healing, and see yourself well. Get to where you dream it, think about it, and it becomes your identity—not what you see with your eyes or feel in your body, but what you see with your heart. When you can see it on the inside, then you'll see it manifest on the outside.

Need prayer?

Please call **719-635-1111** for prayer or for more information on Charis Bible College.

awmi.net | charisbiblecollege.org

GO DEEPER

Self–Examination Questions

What is your attitude toward imagination? How can using your imagination help you receive your healing?

Do you see yourself well, or do you see yourself sick?

Do you dream often? When you dream, do you dream about being healed?

Prayer Points

Use these prayer points to write and to pray your own powerful prayer.

- Thank God for imagination.
- Thank God for not creating sickness.
- Ask God to help you imagine yourself healed.
- Ask God to help you dream, think, and plan like a healed person.
- Ask God to direct you to scriptures to meditate on to help you have hope that turns into faith.
- Thank God for showing you your identity as a healed person.

Action Steps

- In your Healing University journal, write a diary entry imagining yourself totally healed. Explain the things you will do, say, eat, and the places you will go. Plan for the future in your healed existence. Repeat this every day for a week. Then, take a page in your journal and write down any ways you are beginning to see the healing manifest or how you are thinking or dreaming differently about yourself.

- Settle in your heart that your mind can imagine and get a picture on the inside of you that you are healed. As you build your hope into faith, the manifestation will happen in the physical realm. Examine your heart and, when you are ready, make the following declaration and don't waver from it:

  I believe that inside me I will have a picture of myself healed and that it will manifest in the physical realm. _____ (sign and date)

- Make a list of scriptures to meditate on to build hope that will fuel your faith to be healed. Review these verses until you see them growing inside you and painting a picture of you exhibiting your healing.

- Write your own answer to this question: *How will the power of imagination impact healing?*

Want more information on Charis Bible College?

Please call **719-635-1111** for information on Charis Bible College or for prayer.

awmi.net | charisbiblecollege.org

SCRIPTURES

The Power of Imagination

Genesis 6:5 (*KJV*)

> *And God saw that the wickedness of man was great in the earth, and that every imagination of the thoughts of his heart was only evil continually.*

Isaiah 26:3 (*KJV*)

> *Thou wilt keep him in perfect peace, whose mind is stayed on thee: because he trusteth in thee.*

Genesis 11:5–6 (*KJV*)

> *And the Lord came down to see the city and the tower, which the children of men builded. And the Lord said, Behold, the people is one, and they have all one language; and this they begin to do: and now nothing will be restrained from them, which they have imagined to do.*

Proverbs 23:7 (*KJV*)

> *For as he thinketh in his heart, so is he: Eat and drink, saith he to thee; but his heart is not with thee.*

1 Peter 1:23 (*KJV*)

> *Being born again, not of corruptible seed, but of incorruptible, by the word of God, which liveth and abideth for ever.*

John 14:12 (*KJV*)

> *Verily, verily, I say unto you, He that believeth on me, the works that I do shall he do also; and greater works than these shall he do; because I go unto my Father.*

Mark 16:18 (*KJV*)

> *They shall take up serpents; and if they drink any deadly thing, it shall not hurt them; they shall lay hands on the sick, and they shall recover.*

John 11 (*KJV*) – The Death of Lazarus

Luke 7:11–15 (*KJV*)

> And it came to pass the day after, that he went into a city called Nain; and many of his disciples went with him, and much people. Now when he came nigh to the gate of the city, behold, there was a dead man carried out, the only son of his mother, and she was a widow: and much people of the city was with her. And when the Lord saw her, he had compassion on her, and said unto her, Weep not. And he came and touched the bier: and they that bare him stood still. And he said, Young man, I say unto thee, Arise. And he that was dead sat up, and began to speak. And he delivered him to his mother.

Mark 5:35–43 (*KJV*)

> While he yet spake, there came from the ruler of the synagogue's house certain which said, Thy daughter is dead: why troublest thou the Master any further? As soon as Jesus heard the word that was spoken, he saith unto the ruler of the synagogue, Be not afraid, only believe. And he suffered no man to follow him, save Peter, and James, and John the brother of James. And he cometh to the house of the ruler of the synagogue, and seeth the tumult, and them that wept and wailed greatly. And when he was come in, he saith unto them, Why make ye this ado, and weep? the damsel is not dead, but sleepeth. And they laughed him to scorn. But when he had put them all out, he taketh the father and the mother of the damsel, and them that were with him, and entereth in where the damsel was lying. And he took the damsel by the hand, and said unto her, Talitha cumi; which is, being interpreted, Damsel, I say unto thee, arise. And straightway the damsel arose, and walked; for she was of the age of twelve years. And they were astonished with a great astonishment. And he charged them straitly that no man should know it; and commanded that something should be given her to eat.

2 Corinthians 10:3–5 (*KJV*)

> For though we walk in the flesh, we do not war after the flesh: (For the weapons of our warfare are not carnal, but mighty through God to the pulling down of strong holds;) Casting down imaginations, and every high thing that exalteth itself against the knowledge of God, and bringing into captivity every thought to the obedience of Christ;

Genesis 11:6–7 (*KJV*)

> And the Lord said, Behold, the people is one, and they have all one language; and this they begin to do: and now nothing will be restrained from them, which they have imagined to do. Go to, let us go down, and there confound their language, that they may not understand one another's speech.

1 Chronicles 29:18 (*KJV*)

O Lord God of Abraham, Isaac, and of Israel, our fathers, keep this for ever in the imagination of the thoughts of the heart of thy people, and prepare their heart unto thee.

Romans 8:24–25 (*KJV*)

For we are saved by hope: but hope that is seen is not hope: for what a man seeth, why doth he yet hope for? But if we hope for that we see not, then do we with patience wait for it.

2 Corinthians 4:18 (*KJV*)

While we look not at the things which are seen, but at the things which are not seen: for the things which are seen are temporal; but the things which are not seen are eternal.

Mark 11:24 (*KJV*)

Therefore I say unto you, What things soever ye desire, when ye pray, believe that ye receive them, and ye shall have them.

2 Corinthians 5:1 (*KJV*)

For we know that if our earthly house of this tabernacle were dissolved, we have a building of God, an house not made with hands, eternal in the heavens.

2 Corinthians 5:7 (*KJV*)

For we walk by faith, not by sight.

Hebrews 11:1 (*KJV*)

Now faith is the substance of things hoped for, the evidence of things not seen.

1 John 5:4 (*KJV*)

For whatsoever is born of God overcometh the world: and this is the victory that overcometh the world, even our faith.

Psalms 1:1 (*KJV*)

Blessed is the man that walketh not in the counsel of the ungodly, nor standeth in the way of sinners, nor sitteth in the seat of the scornful.

Psalms 2:1 (*KJV*)

Why do the heathen rage, and the people imagine a vain thing?

Isaiah 52:14 (*KJV*)

As many were astonied at thee; his visage was so marred more than any man, and his form more than the sons of men.

Lesson 3
The Power of Attitude
Instructor:
Barry Bennett

Note: All scriptures used in this lesson are quoted from the *New King James Version*.

I. The kind of attitude we have is going to determine the kind of harvest that we reap in our lives.

> *For as he thinks in his heart, so is he. "Eat and drink!" he says to you, But his heart is not with you.*
>
> Proverbs 23:7

A. If you speak negative words—words of fear, words of worry, words of anxiety, words of negativity, words like "it never works out for me and everything always goes wrong"—they're coming from your heart.

> *Brood of vipers! How can you, being evil, speak good things? For out of the abundance of the heart the mouth speaks. A good man out of the good treasure of his heart brings forth good things, and an evil man out of the evil treasure brings forth evil things.*
>
> Matthew 12:34–35

B. Out of the heart you'll bring forth evil things or bring forth good things.

C. Whether we realize it or not, we've made decisions about how good God is, and whether He's really, really good, or just a little bit good, depending on how we do.

II. Everything in our lives is impacted by what goes on inside of our hearts.

> *Keep your heart with all diligence, For out of it* spring *the issues of life.*
>
> Proverbs 4:23

A. The way you approach circumstances, the way you approach relationships, or the way you approach what the doctor told you: those are the issues of life.

B. The image you carry of yourself on the inside of you, and the image you carry of God, is a prophetic picture of your future. You limit yourself and God to the pictures you carry in your imagination.

C. There are many sick Christians who have a vision (an image) of themselves as being sick.

D. If sickness comes against people with healthy hearts and good images of God and themselves, they won't see themselves as sick trying to get well. They see themselves as healed, resisting sickness.

III. Your attitude will determine how you deal with sickness.

A. The kingdom of God within you is being attacked by a sickness that is trying to steal, kill, and destroy your life.

B. We need to attack these problems with faith, with the Word of God, and with the authority of Christ, and not put up with whatever is coming to steal our lives.

IV. The world is trying desperately to conform you to its image, especially in the realm of health.

> *And do not be conformed to this world, but be transformed by the renewing of your mind, that you may prove what is that good and acceptable and perfect will of God.*
> Romans 12:2

A. We need to get stirred up, take back what is ours, take our inheritance in Christ, and not be conformed to this world.

V. If we're going to change our attitudes, we're going to have to start with changing how we think.

> *Finally, brethren, whatever things are true, whatever things are noble, whatever things are just, whatever things are pure, whatever things are lovely, whatever things are of good report, if there is any virtue and if there is anything praiseworthy— meditate on these things. The things which you learned and received and heard and saw in me, these do, and the God of peace will be with you.*
> Philippians 4:8–9

A. You can't be victorious in the area of health and healing if you continually feed yourself with negative thoughts, negative reports, negative garbage on TV, and advertisements for all kinds of medicines with side effects.

B. A joyful heart is an attitude that you must choose in order to overcome the trials and tribulations of life, including sickness. God is rejoicing over you with joy.

A merry heart does good, like *medicine, But a broken spirit dries the bones.*

Proverbs 17:22

C. As your attitude changes, your body will submit to the prevailing thoughts and attitude.

D. We've got to have a more proactive, aggressive attitude that health and healing were purchased for us on the cross and that we're not going to let any enemy steal it from us.

VI. Job shows a negative example of thoughts coming true. He lost his health and his family because he greatly feared all of those events.

For the thing I greatly feared has come upon me, And what I dreaded has happened to me.

Job 3:25

A. Job's fear attracted what he was afraid of, just like faith will attract what we are convinced of.

B. Job didn't have the Word of God to meditate in day and night.

I have heard of You by the hearing of the ear, But now my eye sees You.

Job 42:5

VII. Expectation is an intense anticipation. Hope is intense anticipation of good based upon the promises of God.

According to my earnest expectation and hope that in nothing I shall be ashamed, but with all boldness, as always, so now also Christ will be magnified in my body, whether by life or by death.

Philippians 1:20

A. Faith doesn't come from negative expectations. Faith doesn't grow in the soil of a negative, pessimistic outlook on life, on health, and on God.

Now faith is the substance of things hoped for, the evidence of things not seen.

Hebrews 11:1

B. Your expectation really is where your attitude comes from. Your attitude about life and your expectations about life are powerful, powerful weapons in the world of health and healing.

C. If the grace of healing did overwhelm you, and you got healed, and if negativity was your outlook on life, then you wouldn't stay healed very long. Negativity is the environment for sickness to thrive.

D. Pessimism is the breeding ground for unbelief.

E. Expectations are built on information, memory of how things went in the past, and on how they might go in the future. Expectations are built upon teachings that we've heard and words about God and about ourselves.

F. Based upon experience with five loaves and two fishes in the past, the disciples concluded it wasn't enough for thousands of people. Jesus took the same five loaves and two fishes but had a different expectation, a different vision.

VIII. Our attitudes and expectations come from somewhere. The God of all hope is filling me with joy and peace as I believe, and my belief can only come from the soil of hope.

Now may the God of hope fill you with all joy and peace in believing, that you may abound in hope by the power of the Holy Spirit.

Romans 15:13

A. Multitudes followed Jesus because they expected to be healed. Everybody who came to Jesus was healed.

Also a multitude gathered from the surrounding cities to Jerusalem, bringing sick people and those who were tormented by unclean spirits, and they were all healed.

Acts 5:16

B. A positive expectation is the birthplace of miracles.

C. Faith will only grow in the soil of the intense anticipation of God's goodness.

D. "If it's God's will" is not faith; it is robbing God of the only thing that pleases Him. Without faith it's impossible to please God.

IX. You can change your expectations.

A. Keep the promises of God in front of you.

B. Be aware of your current expectations.

C. Train your mind to think "God thoughts."

X. Make a choice today to change the way you approach life, change your attitude, change your expectations, and give faith a chance.

1. Why is it important to guard your heart?

2. What attitude toward sickness would a person with a healthy heart have?

3. Give a biblical example of negative expectations impacting health.

4. Give a biblical example of positive expectations impacting health.

5. What are three keys to changing your expectations?

6. What cultivates faith to grow so healing will come?

Want more information on
Charis Bible College?

Please call **719-635-1111** for information
on Charis Bible College or for prayer.

awmi.net | charisbiblecollege.org

**LESSON REVIEW
ANSWERS**

1. Why is it important to guard your heart?

    Possible answers: Proverbs 4:23 says the heart is the wellspring of life; from our hearts we express our core beliefs, faith or fear, joy or sadness, peace or stress.

2. What attitude toward sickness would a person with a healthy heart have?

    People with a healthy heart don't see themselves as sick trying to get well. They see themselves as healed resisting sickness.

3. Give a biblical example of negative expectations impacting health.

    Possible answer: Job feared, and his fears happened.

4. Give a biblical example of positive expectations impacting health.

    Possible answer: The multitudes followed Jesus expecting to be healed, and they were all healed.

5. What are three keys to changing your expectations?

    The three keys are: keep the promises of God in front of you; be aware of your current expectations; and train your mind to think "God thoughts."

6. What cultivates faith to grow so healing will come?

    Faith grows with an intense anticipation of good: an outlook on life that is positive and expects the best, expects the favor of God, expects the blessings of God, expects healing and health, expects prosperity, and expects goodness and mercy to follow you all the days of your life.

POINTS TO PONDER

- We all have certain kinds of expectations depending on the input from our culture, from our teachers in school, from our parents, and from our friends. The kinds of input that we have had sown into us form the outlook on life that we have. That outlook will be positive or negative, and it will have a lot of influence on how we walk in health, peace, and relationships.

- The way we think about God, ourselves, the world around us, and the subject of health comes from our hearts. The way we allow our hearts to think or to view life is what we will harvest in life.

- We often speak about ourselves the way we feel about ourselves, and those words and attitudes impact how we live and our health—physical, mental, emotional.

- People who see themselves sick have identified with the sickness, and it has become their new identity. Whereas a well person will have a completely different approach and say, "This shouldn't be."

- Sickness is a snake. It comes to steal, kill, and destroy. But it will live in your house as long as you'll let it.

- The world wants to squeeze you into an image of expectations according to the decade of age in which you are living. They are conforming you to the image of the medical advice they want you to take in each decade of your life.

- The joy of the Lord should be our strength, and we should have an attitude of joy, looking forward to tomorrow and not dreading it.

- Your body is going to begin to conform to the prevailing way that you live your life. It's already being conformed to the negativity, to the fear, to the anxiety, and to the depression. But you can flip it around. This means changing the way you think, changing what comes out of your heart, and changing the words that you speak.

- Your body is a temple of God, and He's given this body to you to care for and to reign over. You become the ruler over your body. You don't wait for your body to tell you you're healed. You tell your body what's up!

- Job didn't have what we have. But we have the Word of God to meditate on day and night and to get our vision, understanding, and hearts changed so that we might have a godly attitude about our lives and against sickness.

- You can't be in faith for your healing if you have a negative outlook on life. It's impossible. The two are contradictory.

- You've already set the parameters of what you'll allow God to heal based upon how you judge yourself.

- Overcomers have gotten a revelation of how good God is and that their worthiness or their righteousness isn't from themselves; it's from God. It's a gift. It's called the gift of righteousness.

- The attitude, "If this is how it used to be, then that's what it's going to be like going forward," discounts the Word of God.

- If you can't go into the abundant promises of God with your own spiritual eyesight, you're not going to have them. You're approaching life the way the disciples approached the loaves and the fish—this isn't enough.

- The multitudes wouldn't have chased after Jesus if He was busy criticizing and judging and rebuking and making fun of people or healing some and not healing others. The reason multitudes followed Jesus was because they expected goodness from Him.

- Your expectation will either be biblical hope, based on the promises of God, or fear and defeat like the rest of the world.

GO DEEPER

Self-Examination Questions

How much of your time do you spend thinking about your sickness? How much of your time do you spend thinking about God and Scripture?

Are you daily looking at the problems of your life, or are you looking at the promises of God? Is there anything you'd change about what you are looking at?

Who is setting your expectations? Are there changes you will make about who you let influence you?

Prayer Points

Use these prayer points to write and to pray your own powerful prayer:

- Thank God for the power and authority of His Word.
- Choose to submit yourself to the Word and let it transform your heart, attitude, vision, and expectations.
- Thank God for the transformation process.
- Refuse to conform to the attitudes and expectations of the world.
- Ask God to help you dig deep within yourself to understand where you get your attitudes and expectations.
- Ask God to help you change who you allow to influence your expectations.
- Choose to have a positive, biblical attitude of an overcomer in Christ.
- Thank God for health and healing in your body.

Action Steps

- In your Healing University journal, write what you are expecting. Be detailed and create a timeline. Are you avoiding future events because of your symptoms, or have you put things on hold because of how you feel? As you begin to navigate your attitude and expectations, you can begin to envision a different future.

- Settle in your heart that your attitude and your expectations are powerful weapons for health and healing. Examine your heart and, when you are ready, make the following declaration and don't waver from it:

I believe God's promises, and I choose to have my attitude and expectations come from God, not the world.

_____ (sign and date)

- Write your own answer to this question: *What is your attitude toward health and healing?*

The Power of Attitude

Proverbs 23:7

For as he thinks in his heart, so is he. "Eat and drink!" he says to you, But his heart is not with you.

Matthew 12:34–35

Brood of vipers! How can you, being evil, speak good things? For out of the abundance of the heart the mouth speaks. A good man out of the good treasure of his heart brings forth good things, and an evil man out of the evil treasure brings forth evil things.

Proverbs 4:23

Keep your heart with all diligence, for out of it spring *the issues of life.*

Romans 12:2

And do not be conformed to this world, but be transformed by the renewing of your mind, that you may prove what is that good and acceptable and perfect will of God.

Philippians 4:8–9

Finally, brethren, whatever things are *true, whatever things* are *noble, whatever things* are *just, whatever things* are *pure, whatever things* are *lovely, whatever things* are *of good report, if* there is *any virtue and if* there is *anything praiseworthy—meditate on these things. The things which you learned and received and heard and saw in me, these do, and the God of peace will be with you.*

Proverbs 17:22

A merry heart does good, like *medicine, But a broken spirit dries the bones.*

Job 3:25

For the thing I greatly feared has come upon me, And what I dreaded has happened to me.

Job 42:5

I have heard of You by the hearing of the ear, But now my eye sees You.

Philippians 1:20

According to my earnest expectation and hope that in nothing I shall be ashamed, but with all boldness, as always, so now also Christ will be magnified in my body, whether by life or by death.

Hebrews 11:1

Now faith is the substance of things hoped for, the evidence of things not seen.

Romans 15:13

Now may the God of hope fill you with all joy and peace in believing, that you may abound in hope by the power of the Holy Spirit.

Acts 5:16

Also a multitude gathered from the surrounding cities to Jerusalem, bringing sick people and those who were tormented by unclean spirits, and they were all healed.

Want more information on Charis Bible College?

Please call **719-635-1111** for information on Charis Bible College or for prayer.

awmi.net | charisbiblecollege.org

Lesson 4
The Power of the Word

Instructor:
Andrew Wommack

Note: All scriptures used in this lesson are quoted from the *King James Version*.

I. The Word of God is an incorruptible seed. The Greek word *spora* is a derivative of the word *sperma*, where we get our English word "sperm." In the same way that a child has to be conceived, you can pray and get healed, but you still have to sow a seed.

> *Being born again, not of corruptible seed, but of incorruptible, by the word of God, which liveth and abideth for ever.*
>
> 1 Peter 1:23, *KJV*

A. The Word of God is what causes us to be born again.

B. A lot of people who pray for a person to be born again think prayer is going to save that person. This scripture doesn't say that you're born again through prayer.

C. Prayer will prepare the soil, break up the fallow ground, put water and fertilizer on it, and cause it to grow. But prayer, if there isn't a seed sown, cannot cause something to grow.

D. Prayer is not going to get a person born again unless the truth of God's Word comes to them.

> *And ye shall know the truth, and the truth shall make you free.*
>
> John 8:32, *KJV*

E. Some people pray for their family members, neighbors, or loved ones to be saved, yet wouldn't dare speak the Word to them. No one will ever be born again by a virgin birth. The Word of God has to be sown, and it's the same way when it comes to healing.

So then faith cometh by hearing, and hearing by the word of God.

Romans 10:17, *KJV*

II. The stronger you are in the Word, the less you will need to have someone else help you because the Word will produce the results that you need.

   A. When you live a scripture, you'll be able to find it. If you have trouble with the address (scripture reference), you'll be able to quote it because that Word has come alive on the inside of you.

III. This physical world operates off the principle of seeds.

   A. All of the life that God created on this planet could not exist without seeds, and in the spiritual realm, there is a comparison that the Word of God is a seed.

IV. The problem has been that we've been focused on things other than the Word of God. The Word of God is health to your flesh.

My son, attend to my words; incline thine ear unto my sayings. Let them not depart from thine eyes; keep them in the midst of thine heart. For they are life unto those that find them, and health to all their flesh.

Proverbs 4:20–22, *KJV*

   A. When Satan starts trying to hit me with something, I just start devouring the Word of God.

   B. Most people think, *Well, I can't help what's happening to me. I can't help how I feel.* Yes, you can.

Keep thy tongue from evil, and thy lips from speaking guile. Depart from evil, and do good; seek peace, and pursue it.

Psalms 34:13–14, *KJV*

   C. Your emotional health is more important than your diet and exercise.

   D. When you get to where you hunger for the Word of God more than you hunger for food, I guarantee you, it'll start producing healing in your body.

Neither have I gone back from the commandment of his lips; I have esteemed the words of his mouth more than my necessary food.

Job 23:12, *KJV*

V. In the natural realm, if you plant seeds, not every one is going to grow. Sometimes a seed doesn't release its power. However, the Bible is an incorruptible seed. It is never the problem.

He sent his word, and healed them, and delivered them from their destructions.

Psalms 107:20, *KJV*

A. Mark 4 has parables about the power of the Word of God, and it compares it to a seed.

1. He cast seed into the ground (Mark 4:3).

2. The seed doesn't do anything until it gets in the ground. The previous parable made it clear that the ground is a person's heart (Mark 4:15).

3. You have to leave the seed there (Mark 4:27).

4. The seed just springs and grows up; he knows not how (Mark 4:27).

B. *I don't understand it.* You don't have to understand it. You just have to cooperate with it and do it.

VI. The seed doesn't have an apple in it or an apple tree in it. But somehow, there is something miraculous in that little seed that when you put it in the ground, it activates what's in the ground to produce fruit.

For the earth bringeth forth fruit of herself; first the blade, then the ear, after that the full corn in the ear.

Mark 4:28, *KJV*

A. There are four different words used to describe creation right in Genesis. The heavens and the earth were created out of nothing and the rest mean to form or to build.

1. God created from nothing (Gen. 1:1).

2. The trees came out of the earth (Gen. 1:11).

3. The animals came out of the earth (Gen. 1: 24).

4. Out of the ground the Lord formed us (Gen. 3:19).

B. You can take a seed, plant it in a desert where the soil has been depleted, and that seed will not yield. It won't produce or it won't yield its total fruit because the ground is where all of that comes from.

C. The earth in Mark 4:28 is talking about your heart. When you got born again, in your spirit you were made complete. You're as perfect as you will ever be in eternity.

D. All you have to do is take this incorruptible seed of God's Word and put it in your heart: meditate on it, think about it, and focus on it. Let that seed stay there, and it will start drawing out of your heart—out of the ground will come this healing power and wisdom—anything that you need. It comes out of you.

E. Mark 4:28 says, *"For the earth bringeth forth fruit of herself . . . "* The phrase *"of herself"* is the Greek word *automatos*, where we get "automatic" or "automatically." This is saying that when the seed is planted, the earth automatically brings forth fruit.

F. I don't understand this, but if you put something in dirt, the ground will start trying to eat it, break it down, draw the life out of it and produce something.

VII. Whatever you put in your heart in abundance is what will grow in your life.

Thou wilt keep him in perfect peace, whose mind is stayed on thee: because he trusteth in thee.

Isaiah 26:3, *KJV*

A. If you aren't in perfect peace, it's because your mind isn't stayed upon Him.

VIII. There are steps and stages to growth. There are different ways that you can receive healing.

And be not conformed to this world: but be ye transformed by the renewing of your mind, that ye may prove what is that good, and acceptable, and perfect, will of God.

Romans 12:2, *KJV*

A. If you receive a healing from another person through their gift, that is the exception rather than the rule.

B. God intended for you to plant the seed in your heart, then let that seed conceive and bring forth healing.

C. If you aren't aware of the stages, then you'll pray and, if you don't have a full manifestation of your healing, get discouraged, thinking that it didn't work or that it just partially worked.

D. Give it a little bit of time and focus on what you have instead of on what you don't have. Focus on the fact that, praise God, it's better.

IX. The Word of God has authority.

A. The Roman centurion in Matthew 8 wasn't Jewish or even what we would call a "Christian." But Jesus said He hadn't ever seen greater faith than his (Matt. 8:10). What made this man's faith so great? His faith was great because he put emphasis on the Word.

When Jesus heard it, he marvelled, and said to them that followed, Verily I say unto you, I have not found so great faith, no, not in Israel.

Matthew 8:10, *KJV*

B. Contrast this centurion's faith with one of Jesus's disciple's unbelief.

But Thomas, one of the twelve, called Didymus, was not with them when Jesus came. The other disciples therefore said unto him, We have seen the Lord. But he said unto them, Except I shall see in his hands the print of the nails, and put my finger into the print of the nails, and thrust my hand into his side, I will not believe.

John 20:24–25, *KJV*

C. Some people cannot believe something that they can't see or touch. They're what the Bible calls carnal. The word *carnal* just means of the five senses. In other words, a carnal person is limited to the five senses, what he can see, taste, hear, smell, and feel.

D. I believe that God created man with six senses, and the sixth sense is faith. Faith is your ability to perceive and see things that you can't see with just your physical eyes.

For we walk by faith, not by sight.

2 Corinthians 5:7, *KJV*

E. Jesus said there was a greater blessing on those who could believe without seeing than on those who believed because they saw.

Jesus saith unto him, Thomas, because thou hast seen me, thou hast believed: blessed are they that have not seen, and yet have believed.

John 20:29, *KJV*

F. Two times Jesus marveled: at the belief of the centurion (Matt. 8:10) and at the unbelief of people in Nazareth (Mark 6:5-6).

And he could there do no mighty work, save that he laid his hands upon a few sick folk, and healed them. And he marvelled because of their unbelief. And he went round about the villages, teaching.

Mark 6:5-6, *KJV*

G. The highest form of faith is when you take what the Word of God says about your healing and you believe it more than what the doctor says, more than what somebody who's looking at you says, more than what you feel, and more than what you think.

X. Faith isn't denying that you have a problem, but it is denying that all you feel is all there is.

(As it is written, I have made thee a father of many nations,) before him whom he believed, even God, who quickeneth the dead, and calleth those things which be not as though they were.

Romans 4:17, *KJV*

A. There are spiritual realities, and there are things that are absolutely forever settled in heaven that may not have totally manifested in your body yet—but that Word is true.

For ever, O LORD, thy word is settled in heaven.

Psalms 119:89, *KJV*

B. The Word is what created everything physical, even your body.

> *In the beginning was the Word, and the Word was with God, and the Word was God. The same was in the beginning with God. All things were made by him; and without him was not any thing made that was made.*
>
> John 1:1–3, *KJV*

C. The Word will exist long after this physical world and this physical body is gone.

> *But the word of the Lord endureth for ever. And this is the word which by the gospel is preached unto you.*
>
> 1 Peter 1:25, *KJV*

D. The Word of God is eternal, and it's more real than what you feel in your body.

> *While we look not at the things which are seen, but at the things which are not seen: for the things which are seen are temporal; but the things which are not seen are eternal.*
>
> 2 Corinthians 4:18, *KJV*

XI. We've got promises upon promises about God's will for us to be well.

A. "God, what You said is true, and I don't care who says anything else."

> *God forbid: yea, let God be true, but every man a liar; as it is written, That thou mightest be justified in thy sayings, and mightest overcome when thou art judged.*
>
> Romans 3:4, *KJV*

B. The seed has to be put in the ground, put in your heart, and left there. It takes a period of time for this to work. It's simple, but it's not easy. You're going to have everything—your senses, your natural mind, and people around you—contradict something that was written in a book thousands of years ago. However, you must base your life more on that Word than on what the doctor says or what your body feels.

C. The Holy Spirit will help you to believe. The Holy Spirit will give you this supernatural, God kind of faith, but He's not going to force it on you. You have to begin the process. You have to reach out and start taking and speaking these truths.

1. What correlation exists between the process of being born again and the process of being healed?

2. What activates growth in a seed?

3. Considering Psalms 107:20, what is one way the Word of God is unlike a natural seed?

4. What did you learn about the power of the ground for the seed that applies to healing?

5. What are the steps and stages of growth for a plant?

6. What are the steps and stages of growth for healing?

7. What is a new aspect of seeing the Word of God as an incorruptible seed that you learned in this lesson?

LESSON REVIEW ANSWERS

1. What correlation exists between the process of being born again and the process of being healed?

    The Word of God has to be planted in someone and then they can be saved. A person can't be healed without the Word of God being sown.

2. What activates growth in a seed?

    The seed has to be planted in the ground. It is the ground that brings forth growth, resulting in a plant.

3. Considering Psalms 107:20, what is one way the Word of God is unlike a natural seed?

    Not all natural seeds work, but God's Word always works.

4. What did you learn about the power of the ground for the seed that applies to healing?

    Possible answer: I learned the ground activates what is already inside the seed to produce what it should, and when the Word of God is placed in my spirit, my faith gets activated.

5. What are the steps and stages of growth for a plant?

    A plant grows when a seed is put in the ground, watered, and left alone for the ground to break down the seed and draw out the life from the seed.

6. What are the steps and stages of growth for healing?

    The steps for healing are to read and plant the Word of God in my spirit and let it conceive through meditating on it. Then I let it grow on the inside of me by focusing on it and believing it above what anyone else says.

7. What is a new aspect of seeing the Word of God as an incorruptible seed that you learned in this lesson?

    Answers will vary.

- You can't be healed without the seed of God's Word being sown.

- The Word of God is to healing as physical seeds are to this physical world. If you want to produce a crop, plant a seed in the ground. If you want a healing, plant the Word in your heart.

- We put so much emphasis on diet and exercise, but we should emphasize the Word of God.

- I believe that spiritual things, specifically focusing on the Word of God, is more important than any physical or natural vitamin, supplement, or health regimen. The Word of God should be your focus.

- God's Word never fails to produce healing. Sometimes we fail to take the Word of God and let it stay on the inside of us, but it's never God's Word that is at fault.

- When God says something to you through the Word, you have to take it, hide it in your heart and leave it there. You can't dig it up or let somebody else dig it up.

- In your spirit, you're complete. You've got everything that you could possibly ever need in your spirit already. You don't need it to come from the outside. It's inside of you, but you do have to activate it.

- Your heart automatically starts producing whatever you focus on.

- God never intended for us to live off of people who have a special anointing on their lives or that we just follow them around, dependent upon them.

- You may not see a complete healing the very first moment. But if you can see any improvements, you ought to say, "Man, that's the blade, and then here comes the ear, and now the full corn in the ear." You just give it some time, and you'll start improving.

- Those who put their faith in the Word, the incorruptible seed, are displaying the greatest exhibition of faith that there is.

- When it comes to healing, many people are controlled by what they feel. They say, "I still feel pain. How can I believe that I am healed?" Faith takes God's Word that says, "by His stripes I am healed" (Is. 53:5) and believes that more than what is felt and more than what the doctor says.

- Believe the Word of God more than anything else.

- You need to say, "I've spoken the Word, and I'm getting better. I don't deny that I still have a little twinge of something, a little pain. I don't deny that I have it, but I deny that that's all there is. The Word of God is more real to me than what I feel in my body."

- You will even have well-meaning people—people who aren't mad at you and who love you but think you're delusional—try to talk you out of it. I tell you what, it's as easy as what I'm saying, but it's one of the hardest things you'll ever do to get to where you *let God be true, but every man a liar"* (Rom. 3:4).

Self–Examination Questions

How would you rate the time you spend meditating on God's Word and getting it inside you to conceive your healing? Are there ways you can improve? How?

What scriptures are you standing on for your healing?

Prayer Points

Use these prayer points to write and pray your own powerful prayer:

- Thank God for His Word.
- Acknowledge that the Word of God is absolutely essential for your healing.
- Thank God that His Word brings health to all of your flesh.
- Thank God that He sent His Word and healed all.
- Thank God that His Word works, even though you don't understand how it works.
- Ask the Holy Spirit to guide you as you meditate on scriptures regarding healing.
- Thank God that His Word will bring healing and activate the supernatural.

Action Steps

- In your Healing University journal, draw a plant or insert a picture. Write at the bottom of the page: "God intended for me to plant the seed of God's Word in my heart. Let that seed conceive and bring forth healing." Around the picture of the plant, write details of scripture references you are planting, things you are saying or doing, or anything that you are already seeing manifest.

- Settle in your heart that the Word of God is the incorruptible seed and that you can't be healed without the seed of God's Word being sown. Examine your heart and, when you are ready, make the following declaration and don't waver from it:

I believe the Word of God more than I believe anything else. I will place that incorruptible seed inside me, meditate on it, and it will activate the supernatural.

_____ (sign and date)

- Write your own answer to this question: *What is your attitude toward the Word of God and your health and healing?*

The Power of the Word

1 Peter 1:23 (*KJV*)

> *Being born again, not of corruptible seed, but of incorruptible, by the word of God, which liveth and abideth for ever.*

John 8:32 (*KJV*)

> *And ye shall know the truth, and the truth shall make you free.*

John 17:17 (*KJV*)

> *Sanctify them through thy truth: thy word is truth.*

Romans 10:17 (*KJV*)

> *So then faith cometh by hearing, and hearing by the word of God.*

1 Peter 2:24 (*KJV*)

> *Who his own self bare our sins in his own body on the tree, that we, being dead to sins, should live unto righteousness: by whose stripes ye were healed.*

Mark 16:18 (*KJV*)

> *They shall take up serpents; and if they drink any deadly thing, it shall not hurt them; they shall lay hands on the sick, and they shall recover.*

James 5:14 (*KJV*)

> *Is any sick among you? let him call for the elders of the church; and let them pray over him, anointing him with oil in the name of the Lord.*

Proverbs 4:20–22 (*KJV*)

> *My son, attend to my words; incline thine ear unto my sayings. Let them not depart from thine eyes; keep them in the midst of thine heart. For they are life unto those that find them, and health to all their flesh.*

Psalms 34:13–14 (*KJV*)

Keep thy tongue from evil, and thy lips from speaking guile. Depart from evil, and do good; seek peace, and pursue it.

Proverbs 17:22 (*KJV*)

A merry heart doeth good like a medicine: but a broken spirit drieth the bones.

Philippians 4:4 (*KJV*)

Rejoice in the Lord always: and again I say, Rejoice.

John 16:33 (*KJV*)

These things I have spoken unto you, that in me ye might have peace. In the world ye shall have tribulation: but be of good cheer; I have overcome the world.

John 14:1 (*KJV*)

Let not your heart be troubled: ye believe in God, believe also in me.

Deuteronomy 28:47–49 (*KJV*)

Because thou servedst not the LORD thy God with joyfulness, and with gladness of heart, for the abundance of all things; Therefore shalt thou serve thine enemies which the LORD shall send against thee, in hunger, and in thirst, and in nakedness, and in want of all things: and he shall put a yoke of iron upon thy neck, until he have destroyed thee. The LORD shall bring a nation against thee from far, from the end of the earth, as swift as the eagle flieth; a nation whose tongue thou shalt not understand;

1 Timothy 4:8 (*KJV*)

For bodily exercise profiteth little: but godliness is profitable unto all things, having promise of the life that now is, and of that which is to come.

Exodus 20:12 (*KJV*)

Honour thy father and thy mother: that thy days may be long upon the land which the LORD thy God giveth thee.

Proverbs 14:30 (*KJV*)

A sound heart is the life of the flesh: but envy the rottenness of the bones.

Job 23:12 (*KJV*)

> *Neither have I gone back from the commandment of his lips; I have esteemed the words of his mouth more than my necessary food.*

Psalms 107:20 (*KJV*)

> *He sent his word, and healed them, and delivered them from their destructions.*

Mark 4:3 (*KJV*)

> *Hearken; Behold, there went out a sower to sow.*

Mark 4:14 (*KJV*)

> *The sower soweth the word.*

Mark 4:15 (*KJV*)

> *And these are they by the way side, where the word is sown; but when they have heard, Satan cometh immediately, and taketh away the word that was sown in their hearts.*

Mark 4:26-29 (*KJV*)

> *And he said, So is the kingdom of God, as if a man should cast seed into the ground; And should sleep, and rise night and day, and the seed should spring and grow up, he knoweth not how. For the earth bringeth forth fruit of herself; first the blade, then the ear, after that the full corn in the ear. But when the fruit is brought forth, immediately he putteth in the sickle, because the harvest is come.*

John 1:1-2 (*KJV*)

> *In the beginning was the Word, and the Word was with God, and the Word was God. The same was in the beginning with God.*

John 6:63 (*KJV*)

> *It is the spirit that quickeneth; the flesh profiteth nothing: the words that I speak unto you, they are spirit, and they are life.*

Genesis 1:1 (*KJV*)

> *In the beginning God created the heaven and the earth.*

Genesis 1:11 (*KJV*)

> And God said, Let the earth bring forth grass, the herb yielding seed, and the fruit tree yielding fruit after his kind, whose seed is in itself, upon the earth: and it was so.

Genesis 1:20 (*KJV*)

> And God said, Let the waters bring forth abundantly the moving creature that hath life, and fowl that may fly above the earth in the open firmament of heaven.

Genesis 1:24 (*KJV*)

> And God said, Let the earth bring forth the living creature after his kind, cattle, and creeping thing, and beast of the earth after his kind: and it was so.

Genesis 1:26 (*KJV*)

> Then God said, "Let Us make man in Our image, according to Our likeness; let them have dominion over the fish of the sea, over the birds of the air, and over the cattle, over all the earth and over every creeping thing that creeps on the earth."

Genesis 2:7 (*KJV*)

> And the Lord God formed man of the dust of the ground, and breathed into his nostrils the breath of life; and man became a living soul.

Genesis 3:19 (*KJV*)

> In the sweat of thy face shalt thou eat bread, till thou return unto the ground; for out of it wast thou taken: for dust thou art, and unto dust shalt thou return.

Ephesians 1:19 (*KJV*)

> And what is the exceeding greatness of his power to us-ward who believe, according to the working of his mighty power.

Colossians 2:10 (*KJV*)

> And ye are complete in him, which is the head of all principality and power.

Isaiah 26:3 (*KJV*)

> Thou wilt keep him in perfect peace, whose mind is stayed on thee: because he trusteth in thee.

Romans 12:2 (*KJV*)

And be not conformed to this world: but be ye transformed by the renewing of your mind, that ye may prove what is that good, and acceptable, and perfect, will of God.

Matthew 8:5–10 (*KJV*)

And when Jesus was entered into Capernaum, there came unto him a centurion, beseeching him, And saying, Lord, my servant lieth at home sick of the palsy, grievously tormented. And Jesus saith unto him, I will come and heal him. The centurion answered and said, Lord, I am not worthy that thou shouldest come under my roof: but speak the word only, and my servant shall be healed. For I am a man under authority, having soldiers under me: and I say to this man, Go, and he goeth; and to another, Come, and he cometh; and to my servant, Do this, and he doeth it. When Jesus heard it, he marvelled, and said to them that followed, Verily I say unto you, I have not found so great faith, no, not in Israel.

John 20:24–25 (*KJV*)

But Thomas, one of the twelve, called Didymus, was not with them when Jesus came. The other disciples therefore said unto him, We have seen the Lord. But he said unto them, Except I shall see in his hands the print of the nails, and put my finger into the print of the nails, and thrust my hand into his side, I will not believe.

2 Corinthians 5:7 (*KJV*)

For we walk by faith, not by sight.

John 20:26–29 (*KJV*)

And after eight days again his disciples were within, and Thomas with them: then came Jesus, the doors being shut, and stood in the midst, and said, Peace be unto you. Then saith he to Thomas, Reach hither thy finger, and behold my hands; and reach hither thy hand, and thrust it into my side: and be not faithless, but believing. And Thomas answered and said unto him, My Lord and my God. Jesus saith unto him, Thomas, because thou hast seen me, thou hast believed: blessed are they that have not seen, and yet have believed.

Mark 6:5–6 (*KJV*)

And he could there do no mighty work, save that he laid his hands upon a few sick folk, and healed them. And he marvelled because of their unbelief. And he went round about the villages, teaching.

Romans 4:17 (*KJV*)

(As it is written, I have made thee a father of many nations,) before him whom he believed, even God, who quickeneth the dead, and calleth those things which be not as though they were.

Psalms 119:89 (*KJV*)

For ever, O LORD, thy word is settled in heaven.

John 1:1–3 (*KJV*)

In the beginning was the Word, and the Word was with God, and the Word was God. The same was in the beginning with God. All things were made by him; and without him was not any thing made that was made.

Colossians 1:16 (*KJV*)

For by him were all things created, that are in heaven, and that are in earth, visible and invisible, whether they be thrones, or dominions, or principalities, or powers: all things were created by him, and for him.

1 Peter 1:25 (*KJV*)

But the word of the Lord endureth for ever. And this is the word which by the gospel is preached unto you.

2 Corinthians 4:18 (*KJV*)

While we look not at the things which are seen, but at the things which are not seen: for the things which are seen are temporal; but the things which are not seen are eternal.

3 John 1:2 (*KJV*)

Beloved, I wish above all things that thou mayest prosper and be in health, even as thy soul prospereth.

Proverbs 4:22 (*KJV*)

For they are life unto those that find them, and health to all their flesh.

Romans 3:4 (*KJV*)

God forbid: yea, let God be true, but every man a liar; as it is written, That thou mightest be justified in thy sayings, and mightest overcome when thou art judged.

Joshua 1:8 (*KJV*)

> *This book of the law shall not depart out of thy mouth; but thou shalt meditate therein day and night, that thou mayest observe to do according to all that is written therein: for then thou shalt make thy way prosperous, and then thou shalt have good success.*

Acts 20:32 (*KJV*)

> *And now, brethren, I commend you to God, and to the word of his grace, which is able to build you up, and to give you an inheritance among all them which are sanctified.*

Lesson 5
The Power of Our Words
Instructor:
Carlie Terradez

Note: All scriptures used in this lesson are quoted from the *New King James Version.*

I.   Words are powerful because they move us at a heart level. The faith to receive healing, or anything that God has for us comes through hearing.

> *So then faith* comes *by hearing, and hearing by the word of God.*
>
> Romans 10:17

A. We need to make sure that we are stocked up on the Word of God, that we are hearing the whole Gospel, and that we are meditating on it because out of the abundance of our hearts our mouths are going to speak.

> *Brood of vipers! How can you, being evil, speak good things? For out of the abundance of the heart the mouth speaks.*
>
> Matthew 12:34

II.   The Word of God talks about the power of our words.

A. Death and life are in the power of our tongues.

> *Death and life* are *in the power of the tongue, And those who love it will eat its fruit.*
>
> Proverbs 18:21

B. That small tongue is powerful enough to change the course of an entire ship.

> *Look also at ships: although they are so large and are driven by fierce winds, they are turned by a very small rudder wherever the pilot desires.*
>
> James 3:4

III. Our tongues are powerful weapons when it comes to the enemy.

    A. Jesus explained the parable: The Word of God is a seed that is being sown. Then He said, "If you don't understand this, basically you're going to struggle to understand all the other parables."

       And again He began to teach by the sea. And a great multitude was gathered to Him, so that He got into a boat and sat in it on the sea; and the whole multitude was on the land facing the sea. Then He taught them many things by parables, and said to them in His teaching: "Listen! Behold, a sower went out to sow. And it happened, as he sowed, that some seed fell by the wayside; and the birds of the air came and devoured it. Some fell on stony ground, where it did not have much earth; and immediately it sprang up because it had no depth of earth. But when the sun was up it was scorched, and because it had no root it withered away. And some seed fell among thorns; and the thorns grew up and choked it, and it yielded no crop. But other seed fell on good ground and yielded a crop that sprang up, increased and produced: some thirtyfold, some sixty, and some a hundred." And He said to them, "He who has ears to hear, let him hear!"

                                                      Mark 4:1–9

    B. Sometimes we think the enemy is just picking on us because he's mean. Well, he is mean, but he's also indiscriminate. He's not really after you; he's after the Word of God that's been implanted in you because Satan understands the power of God's spoken Word.

       The sower sows the word. And these are the ones by the wayside where the word is sown. When they hear, Satan comes immediately and takes away the word that was sown in their hearts. These likewise are the ones sown on stony ground who, when they hear the word, immediately receive it with gladness.

                                                      Mark 4:14–16

    C. Persecution and affliction come to steal the Word from us to try to distract us. You could say that sickness and disease are persecution. They are an affliction, coming to test whether the Word of God or your flesh is more real to you.

       And they have no root in themselves, and so endure only for a time. Afterward, when tribulation or persecution arises for the word's sake, immediately they stumble. Now these are the ones sown among thorns; they are the ones who hear the word, and the cares of this world, the deceitfulness of riches, and the desires for other things entering in choke the word, and it becomes unfruitful.

Mark 4:17–19

D. The words that we listen to are extremely powerful and that's why the enemy wants to get us off track. He will fight for the Word of God not to work in your life.

But these are the ones sown on good ground, those who hear the word, accept it, and bear fruit: some thirtyfold, some sixty, and some a hundred.

Mark 4:20

E. Jesus actually rebuked the enemy with the Word.

Then Jesus was led up by the Spirit into the wilderness to be tempted by the devil. And when He had fasted forty days and forty nights, afterward He was hungry. Now when the tempter came to Him, he said, "If You are the Son of God, command that these stones become bread." But He answered and said, "It is written, 'Man shall not live by bread alone, but by every word that proceeds from the mouth of God.'"

Matthew 4:1–4

IV. The Word of God is how the Lord created the earth in the first place. Words spoken out of our mouths have a creative power.

By faith we understand that the worlds were framed by the word of God, so that the things which are seen were not made of things which are visible.

Hebrews 11:3

A. When Jesus was born, He fulfilled many words, many hundreds of prophecies that were spoken of Him.

B. We need to be speaking into our lives our positive confession. When our confession is the same as what God confesses about our situations, that's powerful!

Seeing then that we have a great High Priest who has passed through the heavens, Jesus the Son of God, let us hold fast our confession.

Hebrews 4:14

C. If we were to apply this to healing, we could put it like this, "Well, the Word of God spoken out of my mouth is powerful; therefore, I'm going to start speaking over my body what Jesus says about my body."

He sent His word and healed them, and delivered them from their destructions.

Psalms 107:20

D. Sometimes we don't realize we have power in our words. But our bodies are listening to us as we speak.

V. God's Word spoken in our mouths is just as powerful as if He'd spoken it Himself.

And I have put My words in your mouth; I have covered you with the shadow of My hand, That I may plant the heavens, Lay the foundations of the earth, And say to Zion, 'You are My people.'"

Isaiah 51:16

A. God will use His spoken words coming out of your mouth to bring peace, to bring joy, and to accomplish and prosper the things for which He sent it.

So shall My word be that goes forth from My mouth; It shall not return to me void, But it shall accomplish what I please, And it shall prosper in the thing for which I sent it.

Isaiah 55:11

B. In the same way that Satan tempted Jesus while He was in the flesh, Satan will tempt us while we're in the flesh. But like Jesus, when we understand that God puts His words in our mouths, and the power that they contain when we deliver them, we can get on board with the Word of God over our situation, and we can see miraculous power delivered.

VI. We can literally change the trajectory of our lives simply with our words.

A. Every promise that's written in the Bible is going to come to pass in our lives when we choose to let it leave our mouths.

This Book of the Law shall not depart from your mouth, but you shall meditate in it day and night, that you may observe to do according to all that is written in it. For then you will make your way prosperous, and then you will have good success. Have I not commanded you? Be strong and of good courage; do not be afraid, nor be dismayed, for the LORD your God is with you wherever you go.

Joshua 1:8–9

B. The word "mouth" in this verse means to speak it as in a commandment. The word "meditate" means to speak it, to study it, to utter it, or roar it like a lion.

C. Jesus was using the power of His words to curse a deceptive fig tree. The enemy might be real, but his weapons are fake. He's a fraud. He's a deceiver, and Jesus couldn't bear to be around deception, so he cursed the fig tree.

In response Jesus said to it, "Let no one eat fruit from you ever again." And His disciples heard it.

Mark 11:14

D. Even though Jesus released power in His words immediately, it took a period of time to see the effects of those words because the word was having an effect on an area that was below the ground.

Now in the morning, as they passed by, they saw the fig tree dried up from the roots.

Mark 11:20

E. We too can release faith and power through our words, and immediately those words will have an effect. But like the fig tree, sometimes there is a period of time before we see the effects of those words manifest in our natural world or manifest on the outside of our bodies.

F. When we take something by faith, we put more trust and confidence (more faith) in what the Word of God says about our situation than how we feel about it, what it looks like, or what the doctor's report says.

For to be carnally minded is death, but to be spiritually minded is life and peace.

Romans 8:6

VII. Have faith in God.

> *For assuredly, I say to you, whoever says to this mountain, "Be removed and be cast into the sea," and does not doubt in his heart, but believes that those things he says will be done, he will have whatever he says. Therefore I say to you, whatever things you ask when you pray, believe that you receive them, and you will have them.*
>
> Mark 11:23–24

  A. *"For assuredly, I say to you . . ."*

   1. This first use of the word *"says"* is a command. The Greek word *epo* means to speak as in a commandment. Jesus is saying, "Speak to the mountain!"

  B. *"Those things he says will be done."*

   1. The second *"says"* is the word *laleó*, meaning to speak out, to use your own voice, and to be bold.

  C. *"Therefore I say to you . . ."*

   1. This word *"say"* is *lego*, and it actually means a systematic set or discourse or the building blocks of life. We'll be measured by our confession and our tenacity to hold fast to that confession.

VIII. We're not speaking to try to convince ourselves to believe something; we're believing, therefore, we're speaking.

> *And since we have the same spirit of faith, according to what is written, "I believed and therefore I spoke," we also believe and therefore speak.*
>
> 2 Corinthians 4:13

  A. You need to start confessing God's Word over your life and holding fast to your confession, speaking what Jesus is saying about your body today.

> *(As it is written, "I have made you a father of many nations") in the presence of Him whom he believed—God, who gives life to the dead and calls those things which do not exist as though they did.*
>
> Romans 4:17

IX. God planned for you before there was even a world for you to live in. Now He's put His voice, His words, His power in your mouth: power to speak out life, to speak out death, to release faith, to release authority, and to rebuke the power of the enemy from working in your body. But He needs your cooperation!

**LESSON REVIEW
QUESTIONS**

1. What does the Word of God say about the power of our words?

2. What does the Parable of the Sower (Mark 4:1–20) teach us about words?

3. What is the creative power of words?

4. According to Isaiah 55:11, why should you be responsible for speaking God's Word out of your mouth?

5. What can we learn about our words from Jesus cursing the fig tree (Mark 11:12–14 and Matt. 21:18–22)?

6. What does Mark 11:23–24 teach about how to speak?

7. What do you feel needs to change about how you speak?

LESSON REVIEW ANSWERS

1. What does the Word of God say about the power of our words?

   Possible answers: Proverbs 18:21 points out that death and life are in the power of the tongue and we get what we speak; James 3:4 reminds us that a ship is turned by a small rudder, and our tongues are small but powerful.

2. What does the Parable of the Sower (Mark 4:1–20) teach us about words?

   Possible answers: The enemy knows the power of God's spoken Word and tries to steal it from us; the words we listen to are powerful; we can use our words to rebuke the enemy.

3. What is the creative power of words?

   Possible answers: God created everything by speaking; Jesus's birth fulfilled the spoken prophecies about Him; we can speak and confess what God says about our health to change our situation.

4. According to Isaiah 55:11, why should you be responsible for speaking God's Word out of your mouth?

   Possible answers: The spoken words of God coming out of your mouth will bring peace and joy and accomplish the things for which He sent it; when I speak God's Word, it is as powerful to create or destroy as when God speaks them.

5. What can we learn about our words from Jesus cursing the fig tree (Mark 11:12–14 and Matt. 21:18–22)?

   Possible answers: Jesus used the power of His words to curse the fig tree; Jesus's words immediately released power, but the results weren't seen immediately.

6.   What does Mark 11:23–24 teach about how to speak?

We can use our words as a command, as bold speech, and as a confession of what Jesus says about the situation.

7.   What do you feel needs to change about how you speak?

Answers will vary.

POINTS TO PONDER

- Not only do you need to be listening to and careful of what words come out of your mouth, you also need to be listening to and careful of what words you're allowing into your mind.

- God has put His Word in your mouth, and when it's spoken out, you can use it against the lies of the enemy.

- Satan can't stop you from receiving the Word of God, but he will do everything in his power to distract you from putting it into practice, mixing it with faith, and bearing fruit in your life. He's terrified that you might just take the Word of God and believe it.

- The enemy is coming to steal the Word from you because he doesn't want it to become fruitful in you.

- Just like the world itself was created by the power of words, when words are spoken out of your mouth, they're powerful. You need to be careful what things are coming out of your mouth.

- If God has the blueprint for your life and you're broken, then He can fix what's broken.

- You need to be responsible for your words and understand that when you speak the Word of God out of your mouth, it's just as powerful to create or to destroy as if God Himself had said it.

- You need to be speaking the Word of God with boldness because its power is released when you speak. Roaring the Word of God and declaring everything in it over your life will cause situations to start to change.

- Faith is simply a trusting confidence in the Word of God, understanding what the Word of God says about your situation, and letting it be more real to you than your five senses.

- You can guarantee that your words have power, but sometimes they're having an effect in an area that cannot be seen by your natural eyes in that moment, so you take it by faith.

- We sow a seed of faith, and then we get a big shovel of unbelief and dig up the seed to see if it's growing. Then we wonder why it doesn't grow.

- "I'm not going to ask God to come and move a mountain that He's already told me to move."

- You can speak the Word of God with boldness.

- God wouldn't have sent His Word and healed you if He didn't want you to be well; He knows how powerful those words are.

- F.F. Bosworth put it this way, "Your success and usefulness in this world will be measured by your confession and your tenacity to hold fast to that confession."

- "I'm not so worried about my speaking as I am about my believing; if I get my believing right, my speaking's going to follow."

- God needs your cooperation to speak out and to speak to the mountains that are in your life.

Need prayer?

Please call **719-635-1111** for prayer or for more information on Charis Bible College.

awmi.net | charisbiblecollege.org

GO DEEPER

Self-Examination Questions

What words and lies has the enemy been speaking to you? What Words of God can you speak against each lie?

What words have you been speaking about your health? Have you been wishfully speaking them or commanding them in Jesus' name?

What personal examples do you have of the power of your words, either positive or negative?

What do you think will be different if you monitor the words you speak closely? How will monitoring your words affect others?

Prayer Points

Use these prayer points to write and to pray your own powerful prayer:

- Thank God for the power of His Word.
- Commit to speak out the Word of God over your life.
- Take authority over sickness and disease.
- Release the power and authority in Jesus' name.
- Command sickness and disease to go.
- Thank God that He sent His Word and healed you.
- Believe and receive healing right now.
- Call the things that be not as though they are.
- Call healing into existence right now.
- Acknowledge the power of God's Word in your mouth.
- Praise God that He is a healing God.

Action Steps

- In your Healing University journal, write down the words you have typically been saying about your situation. Draw an arrow from the words and write down what God's Word says and what you will command boldly and confess about your situation from now on. Begin the pattern now of speaking life and tear down strongholds as you call those things that are not as though they are.

- Next, draw an outline of a body and on the inside write the things that are happening inside your body because of the words you are speaking over your body. Draw speech bubbles showing what your mouth is speaking out. Use this as a reminder that you can't see what is happening inside, but you know the power of God's Word spoken in your mouth, and you have faith that change is happening!

- Settle in your heart that the Word of God spoken from your mouth has power. Examine your heart and, when you are ready, make the following declaration and don't waver from it:

  I believe the Word of God spoken from my mouth has power and authority to alter my situation. _____ (sign and date)

- Write your own answer to this question: *What words do I want to speak to my body about my healing?*

Want more information on Charis Bible College?

Please call **719-635-1111** for information on Charis Bible College or for prayer.

awmi.net | charisbiblecollege.org

SCRIPTURES

The Power of Our Words

Romans 10:17

So then faith comes by hearing, and hearing by the word of God.

Matthew 12:34

Brood of vipers! How can you, being evil, speak good things? For out of the abundance of the heart the mouth speaks.

Proverbs 18:21

Death and life are in the power of the tongue, And those who love it will eat its fruit.

James 3:4

Look also at ships: although they are so large and are driven by fierce winds, they are turned by a very small rudder wherever the pilot desires.

Mark 4:1–9

And again He began to teach by the sea. And a great multitude was gathered to Him, so that He got into a boat and sat in it on the sea; and the whole multitude was on the land facing the sea. Then He taught them many things by parables, and said to them in His teaching: "Listen! Behold, a sower went out to sow. And it happened, as he sowed, that some seed fell by the wayside; and the birds of the air came and devoured it. Some fell on stony ground, where it did not have much earth; and immediately it sprang up because it had no depth of earth. But when the sun was up it was scorched, and because it had no root it withered away. And some seed fell among thorns; and the thorns grew up and choked it, and it yielded no crop. But other seed fell on good ground and yielded a crop that sprang up, increased and produced: some thirtyfold, some sixty, and some a hundred." And He said to them, "He who has ears to hear, let him hear!"

Luke 8:4–8

And when a great multitude had gathered, and they had come to Him from every city, He spoke by a parable: "A sower went out to sow his seed. And as he sowed, some fell by the wayside; and it was trampled down, and the birds of the air devoured it. Some fell on rock; and as soon as it sprang up, it withered away because it lacked moisture. And some fell among thorns, and the thorns sprang up with it and choked it. But others fell on good ground, sprang up, and yielded a crop a hundredfold." When He had said these things He cried, "He who has ears to hear, let him hear!"

Matthew 13:3–9

Then He spoke many things to them in parables, saying: "Behold, a sower went out to sow. And as he sowed, some seed fell by the wayside; and the birds came and devoured them. Some fell on stony places, where they did not have much earth; and they immediately sprang up because they had no depth of earth. But when the sun was up they were scorched, and because they had no root they withered away. And some fell among thorns, and the thorns sprang up and choked them. But others fell on good ground and yielded a crop: some a hundredfold, some sixty, some thirty. He who has ears to hear, let him hear!"

Mark 4:14–20

The sower sows the word. And these are the ones by the wayside where the word is sown. When they hear, Satan comes immediately and takes away the word that was sown in their hearts. These likewise are the ones sown on stony ground who, when they hear the word, immediately receive it with gladness; and they have no root in themselves, and so endure only for a time. Afterward, when tribulation or persecution arises for the word's sake, immediately they stumble. Now these are the ones sown among thorns; they are the ones who hear the word, and the cares of this world, the deceitfulness of riches, and the desires for other things entering in choke the word, and it becomes unfruitful. But these are the ones sown on good ground, those who hear the word, accept it, and bear fruit: some thirtyfold, some sixty, and some a hundred."

Matthew 4:1–4

Then Jesus was led up by the Spirit into the wilderness to be tempted by the devil. And when He had fasted forty days and forty nights, afterward He was hungry. Now when the tempter came to Him, he said, "If You are the Son of God, command that these stones become bread." But He answered and said, "It is written, 'Man shall not live by bread alone, but by every word that proceeds from the mouth of God.'"

Matthew 4:7

Jesus said to him, "It is written again, 'You shall not tempt the LORD your God.'"

Matthew 4:10

Then Jesus said to him, "Away with you, Satan! For it is written, 'You shall worship the LORD your God, and Him only you shall serve.'"

Hebrews 11:3

By faith we understand that the worlds were framed by the word of God, so that the things which are seen were not made of things which are visible.

Hebrews 4:14

Seeing then that we have a great High Priest who has passed through the heavens, Jesus the Son of God, let us hold fast our confession.

Psalms 107:20

He sent His word and healed them, and delivered them from their destructions.

Isaiah 51:16

And I have put My words in your mouth; I have covered you with the shadow of My hand, That I may plant the heavens, Lay the foundations of the earth, And say to Zion, 'You are My people.'"

Isaiah 55:11

So shall My word be that goes forth from My mouth; It shall not return to me void, But it shall accomplish what I please, And it shall prosper in the thing for which I sent it.

Hebrews 4:15

For we do not have a High Priest who cannot sympathize with our weaknesses, but was in all points tempted as we are, yet without sin.

Joshua 1:8–9

This Book of the Law shall not depart from your mouth, but you shall meditate in it day and night, that you may observe to do according to all that is written in it.

For then you will make your way prosperous, and then you will have good success. Have I not commanded you? Be strong and of good courage; do not be afraid, nor be dismayed, for the LORD your God is with you wherever you go.

Mark 11:14

In response Jesus said to it, "Let no one eat fruit from you ever again." And His disciples heard it.

Mark 11:20

Now in the morning, as they passed by, they saw the fig tree dried up from the roots.

Matthew 21:18–19

Now in the morning, as He returned to the city, He was hungry. And seeing a fig tree by the road, He came to it and found nothing on it but leaves, and said to it, "Let no fruit grow on you ever again." Immediately the fig tree withered away.

Romans 8:6

For to be carnally minded is death, but to be spiritually minded is life and peace.

Mark 11:22–24

And Peter, remembering, said to Him, "Rabbi, look! The fig tree which You cursed has withered away." So Jesus answered and said to them, "Have faith in God. For assuredly, I say to you, whoever says to this mountain, "Be removed and be cast into the sea," and does not doubt in his heart, but believes that those things he says will be done, he will have whatever he says. Therefore I say to you, whatever things you ask when you pray, believe that you receive them, and you will have them.

2 Corinthians 4:13

And since we have the same spirit of faith, according to what is written, "I believed and therefore I spoke," we also believe and therefore speak.

Romans 4:17

(As it is written, "I have made you a father of many nations") in the presence of Him whom he believed—God, who gives life to the dead and calls those things which do not exist as though they did.

Romans 4:18–21

> Who, contrary to hope, in hope believed, so that he became the father of many nations, according to what was spoken, "So shall your descendants be." And not being weak in faith, he did not consider his own body, already dead (since he was about a hundred years old), and the deadness of Sarah's womb. He did not waver at the promise of God through unbelief, but was strengthened in faith, giving glory to God, and being fully convinced that what He had promised He was also able to perform.

Isaiah 54:17

> No weapon formed against you shall prosper, And every tongue which rises against you in judgment You shall condemn. This is the heritage of the servants of the LORD, And their righteousness is from Me," Says the LORD.

Lesson 6
Grace for Receiving Healing

Instructor:
Duane Sheriff

Note: All scriptures used in this lesson are quoted from the *New King James Version.*

I. On the same cross that Jesus died for our sins and made righteousness available, He died also for our sicknesses and made healing available.

   A. It's God's grace through faith that has saved you. You can't do anything, quit anything, or start anything to get God to save you. You are saved by God's amazing grace through childlike faith.

   B. It's also true that you can't do anything to get healed.

II. God's grace through faith is how we receive healing, just like God's grace to be saved through faith is how we enter into eternal life.

   A. David celebrated the grace of God. David encouraged us to remember the benefits of God, and yet so many Christians today live far short of the provisions and benefits that God has made available.

   Bless the LORD, O my soul; And all that is within me, bless His holy name! Bless the LORD, O my soul, And forget not all His benefits: Who forgives all your iniquities, Who heals all your diseases, Who redeems your life from destruction, Who crowns you with lovingkindness and tender mercies.

   Psalms 103:1–4

   B. We're not to forget that we're forgiven of all of our iniquities, that God has already extended complete and total forgiveness to every believer, or that our sins—past tense, present tense, and even future tense—have been forgiven by God.

   C. I am a forgiven man. Yet if I sin, I confess that to God, and He cleanses me in my soul where sin affects me emotionally. He also cleanses me in my body, which isn't yet redeemed and where sin can affect me and open up the door for Satan to steal, kill, and destroy.

III. God wills for you to be healed. He wills for you to receive of His love and mercy in this area of your life as well as in the area of forgiveness of sin.

> *Who Himself bore our sins in His own body on the tree, that we, having died to sins, might live for righteousness—by whose stripes you were healed.*
>
> 1 Peter 2:24

A. Jesus bore all your sins and sicknesses 2,000 years ago in His body on the tree, so by His stripes you're now healed. Yet that doesn't mean it's impossible for you to experience sickness in your body.

B. You are healed, and now sickness and disease may be fighting against you in your body, but you can resist sickness just like you can resist sin.

C. Understanding the grace of God helps you fight sickness from a position of victory, not of defeat, as a victim.

D. If you commit a sin or a transgression, that is not your nature, that is not who you are. You can reckon yourself dead to it and alive unto Jesus and live unto righteousness—that's the grace of God (1 Pet. 2:24).

E. You are dead to sickness, and you now need to live unto healing.

   1. Being dead to sickness doesn't mean you never get sick or that it's impossible for you to be tempted with sickness.

   2. It doesn't mean when you're dead to sin that it's impossible for you to sin.

   3. It means sickness has no more power over you than sin has over you.

   4. You can resist sin now because you're righteous in Jesus and live a righteous life by the power of God.

   5. You can resist sickness now, and by the same cross, the same power and grace of God, you can live in healing now.

IV. Without God, sickness is just a part of the human condition.

A. Sickness is just a part of this life and people yield to it, even expect it; many people don't understand that they're believing for it and expecting it.

B. God wants you to believe for healing and expect it when you're tempted to be sick.

V. Sickness was a curse under the Old Covenant law.

> *Christ has redeemed us from the curse of the law, having become a curse for us (for it is written, "Cursed is everyone who hangs on a tree"), that the blessing of Abraham might come upon the Gentiles in Christ Jesus, that we might receive the promise of the Spirit through faith.*
>
> Galatians 3:13–14

A. God did bring sickness as a punishment and as a curse for breaking the Old Testament law. Everywhere under the Old Covenant law you see God putting diseases on and afflicting people, it was His wrath for sin.

B. Christ redeemed us from the curse of the law; He redeemed us from all of those sicknesses, all of those diseases—that is the grace of God.

C. Paul talked about how foolish these Galatians were, how they were saved by grace but then tried to be mature or perfected or live holy by their own works. He tried to bring them back to grace and faith. They were saved by grace, forgiven by grace, and made righteous by grace through faith.

> *O foolish Galatians! Who has bewitched you that you should not obey the truth, before whose eyes Jesus Christ was clearly portrayed among you as crucified? This only I want to learn from you: Did you receive the Spirit by the works of the law, or by the hearing of faith? Are you so foolish? Having begun in the Spirit, are you now being made perfect by the flesh? Have you suffered so many things in vain—if indeed it was in vain?*
>
> Galatians 3:1–4

D. You can't get saved by works of the law and you can't get healed by works of the law. We can't perform miracles among us by works of the law.

> *Therefore He who supplies the Spirit to you and works miracles among you, does He do it by the works of the law, or by the hearing of faith?*
>
> Galatians 3:5

E. Just like people are tempted to try to earn their salvation, people are tempted to try to earn their healing. That's works of the law—that's you appealing to your own holiness.

F. God is reminding us that—just like we are made righteous by grace through faith, and we are forgiven by grace through faith—we are healed by grace through faith.

Just as Abraham "believed God, and it was accounted to him for righteousness."

Galatians 3:6

VI. Sin is connected by some degree to sickness in the world.

Is anyone among you sick? Let him call for the elders of the church, and let them pray over him, anointing him with oil in the name of the Lord. And the prayer of faith will save the sick, and the Lord will raise him up. And if he has committed sins, he will be forgiven.

James 5:14–15

A. By sin, death came into the world. All that makes up death, sickness, disease, oppression, and depression is part of the darkness of this world.

Therefore, just as through one man sin entered the world, and death through sin, and thus death spread to all men, because all sinned.

Romans 5:12

B. The disciples knew there was a connection between sin and sickness; they simply misapplied that connection. It wasn't the personal sins of the baby or the parents that made him blind; it was sin in the world.

Now as Jesus *passed by, He saw a man who was blind from birth. And His disciples asked Him, saying, "Rabbi, who sinned, this man or his parents, that he was born blind?" Jesus answered, "Neither this man nor his parents sinned, but that the works of God should be revealed in him. I must work the works of Him who sent Me while it is day;* the *night is coming when no one can work.*

John 9:1–4

C. Personal sin and living in sin can give place to Satan and create sickness and disease in our lives, but not everybody who is sick personally sinned to cause that sickness or disease. We are born into this fallen world.

D. While Jesus is tarrying His return, our bodies are subject to sickness and disease because they are not redeemed. They've been purchased, they've been bought, and they belong to God, but they're corruptible. So, if we choose to live in sin and rebel against God, we're giving place to Satan, and he came to steal, kill, and destroy.

The thief does not come except to steal, and to kill, and to destroy. I have come that they may have life, and that they may have it more abundantly.

John 10:10

E. We become servants to whoever we yield to. If we yield to Satan in sin, he can bring sickness and disease.

Do you not know that to whom you present yourselves slaves to obey, you are that one's slaves whom you obey, whether of sin leading to death, or of obedience leading to righteousness?

Romans 6:16

VII. God's not going to hold sin against you, and God's not going to withhold healing from you, even if you're falling short in some areas.

A. There is a place to be humble and confess a fault or a trespass to one another, and there's a healing that comes through confession. That includes more than just healing of our bodies.

Confess your trespasses to one another, and pray for one another, that you may be healed. The effective, fervent prayer of a righteous man avails much.

James 5:16

B. A righteous man is a man who has put his faith in the amazing grace of God and been forgiven of his sins. Elijah wasn't a perfect man; he was a man just like us, with shortcomings, but when he prayed in faith, he saw miracles.

C. Receive your healing based on what Jesus did, not what you do, haven't done, or wish you had done. Receive your healing by grace through faith, not works of the law.

1. What is the correlation between salvation and healing?

2. What role does faith have?

3. How does Psalms 103:1–4 relate to the grace of God?

4. Does God's grace mean you'll never be sick? Why or why not?

5. If God brought sickness as a punishment under the Old Covenant, is He bringing sickness on people today? Explain your answer.

6. What role does sin play in your health?

7. After understanding God's grace, how will you receive your healing?

**LESSON REVIEW
ANSWERS**

1.   What is the correlation between salvation and healing?

     Possible answers: I can't earn my salvation, and I can't earn my healing; Jesus died on the cross for my sins and for my sicknesses, so I'm forgiven and healed.

2.   What role does faith have?

     We receive healing by grace through faith, just like we enter into eternal life by grace through faith.

3.   How does Psalms 103:1–4 relate to the grace of God?

     Possible answers: David encourages us to remember the benefits of God; God has forgiven our sins and healed us because of what Christ did on the cross.

4.   Does God's grace mean you'll never be sick? Why or why not?

     Possible answer: No; I'm forgiven and righteous, but because sin exists, so does sickness. I'm not a victim of sickness. Because of the grace of God, I'm fighting sickness from a position of victory.

5.   If God brought sickness as a punishment under the Old Covenant, is He bringing sickness on people today? Explain your answer.

     Possible answer: God afflicted people because of sin under the Old Covenant. Jesus redeemed us from the curse of the law because He redeemed us from sin (Gal. 3:13–14). Jesus wouldn't be healing all if God was still putting sickness on people—Jesus wouldn't go against what God was doing.

6.   What role does sin play in your health?

     Possible answers: God isn't going to withhold healing because of sin, but it can open a door for Satan to bring sickness into my life; when we confess our faults to one another, it opens the door for healing in our bodies and relationships.

7. After understanding God's grace, how will you receive your healing?

I receive my healing by grace through faith in what Jesus did.

POINTS TO PONDER

- One of the reasons people lose the "amazing" in regard to God's grace is they don't see people's lives being changed.

- We can no more be healed by our works than we can be saved by our works.

- The grace that brings forgiveness to you and that you receive by faith is the same grace that makes healing available to you. It too must be received by faith.

- The cross where Jesus bore your sins is the same cross where He bore your sicknesses.

- You have to act on your faith. There are works of faith, but you don't get healed by works of the law any more than you get saved by works of the law.

- God, in grace, has extended forgiveness to you. If or when you sin, you need to run to Him and confess that sin. Sin has consequences horizontally in your life, even though vertically God has accepted, forgiven, and loved you unconditionally.

- You receive forgiveness by standing on the righteousness that Jesus provided for you—that's a benefit.

- You may be tempted to get sick, and you may have symptoms of sickness trying to get in your body, but resist them and fight it just like you would sin. Believe you are healed by the stripes of Jesus and begin to receive it by faith.

- You're not the sick, depressed, deprived, and diseased that's trying to do something to get God to heal you. You're the healed in Jesus whom the devil is trying to make sick. Resist sickness by faith.

- God healed you and made you whole in Jesus. He wants you to live free from sickness.

- A lot of people misunderstand the law, curses, punishment, and wrath of God revealed under the law. They think somehow God is making them sick or that God is punishing them for their sins.

- If you believe God is making you sick to teach you something, then why are you taking medicine and resisting the work of God?

- We pray for people and they get healed, not because we're holy or doing things perfectly, but because Jesus lives in our hearts. It's because of grace on us and because we're believing and exercising faith in Jesus.

- The truth is, you've already got all of heaven itself in the amazing grace of God.

- Many people suffer from sickness and disease and being handicapped, not because God did or willed it, but because of sin in the world.

- If you yield to and obey God, it doesn't mean you won't be tempted with sickness. There still is the possibility of your body having an issue, and you will have to trust God.

- You are a righteous man or a righteous woman if you understand that by God's grace you're saved and you've believed in the grace of God. As a righteous man or woman in Christ, your prayers avail much.

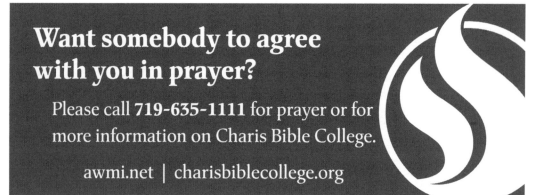

GO DEEPER

Self-Examination Questions

What is your definition of grace? How does that apply to healing?

Why is it important to grasp the true meaning of God's grace?

Are there areas of your life where you accept grace and areas where you do not accept grace? Why? What will it take for you reach a point where you accept grace for healing?

Prayer Points

Use these prayer points to write and to pray your own powerful prayer:

- Thank God for His goodness and grace.
- Ask God to help you continue to grow in your understanding of His grace for your life and for your health.
- Confess areas where you have done something to try to earn forgiveness or healing.
- Acknowledge that sin exists but proclaim your righteousness through Christ.
- Praise Jesus that on the cross He purchased your forgiveness of sins and your healing.
- Praise God that you can stand on amazing grace for your salvation and your healing.

Action Steps

- In your Healing University journal, write a thank you note to God for His grace. Detail what that grace looks like in your life and what impact it has on your health, now that you clearly understand it.

- Settle in your heart that God's amazing grace freely gives you healing through what Jesus has already done on the cross. God's grace through faith is how you received healing, just like God's grace to be saved through faith is how you enter into eternal life. Examine your heart and, when you are ready, make the following declaration and don't waver from it:

I believe that I receive my healing by grace through faith, not by works of the law.

_____ _____ (sign and date)

- Write your own answer to this question: *What does "grace for receiving my healing" mean?*

SCRIPTURES

Grace for Receiving Healing

Psalms 103:1–4

Bless the Lord, *O my soul; and all that is within me,* bless *His holy name! Bless the* Lord, *O my soul, and forget not all His benefits: who forgives all your iniquities, who heals all your diseases, who redeems your life from destruction, who crowns you with lovingkindness and tender mercies.*

1 John 1:9

If we confess our sins, He is faithful and just to forgive us our *sins and to cleanse us from all unrighteousness.*

1 Peter 2:24

Who Himself bore our sins in His own body on the tree, that we, having died to sins, might live for righteousness—by whose stripes you were healed.

1 Peter 2:23

Who, when He was reviled, did not revile in return; when He suffered, He did not threaten, but committed Himself *to Him who judges righteously.*

Galatians 3:13–14

Christ has redeemed us from the curse of the law, having become a curse for us (for it is written, "Cursed is everyone who hangs on a tree"), *that the blessing of Abraham might come upon the Gentiles in Christ Jesus, that we might receive the promise of the Spirit through faith.*

Galatians 3:1–4

O foolish Galatians! Who has bewitched you that you should not obey the truth, before whose eyes Jesus Christ was clearly portrayed among you as crucified? This only I want to learn from you: Did you receive the Spirit by the works of the law, or by the hearing of faith? Are you so foolish? Having begun in the Spirit, are you now being made perfect by the flesh? Have you suffered so many things in vain—if indeed it was in vain?

Galatians 3:5

Therefore He who supplies the Spirit to you and works miracles among you, does He do it *by the works of the law, or by the hearing of faith?*

Galatians 3:6

Just as Abraham "believed God, and it was accounted to him for righteousness."

James 5:14–15

Is anyone among you sick? Let him call for the elders of the church, and let them pray over him, anointing him with oil in the name of the Lord. And the prayer of faith will save the sick, and the Lord will raise him up. And if he has committed sins, he will be forgiven.

Romans 5:12

Therefore, just as through one man sin entered the world, and death through sin, and thus death spread to all men, because all sinned.

John 9:1–4

Now as Jesus *passed by, He saw a man who was blind from birth. And His disciples asked Him, saying, "Rabbi, who sinned, this man or his parents, that he was born blind?" Jesus answered, "Neither this man nor his parents sinned, but that the works of God should be revealed in him. I must work the works of Him who sent Me while it is day;* the *night is coming when no one can work.*

John 10:10

The thief does not come except to steal, and to kill, and to destroy. I have come that they may have life, and that they may have it more abundantly.

Romans 6:16

Do you not know that to whom you present yourselves slaves to obey, you are that one's slaves whom you obey, whether of sin leading to death, or of obedience leading to righteousness?

James 5:16

Confess your trespasses to one another, and pray for one another, that you may be healed. The effective, fervent prayer of a righteous man avails much.

James 5:17–20

Elijah was a man with a nature like ours, and he prayed earnestly that it would not rain; and it did not rain on the land for three years and six months. And he prayed again, and the heaven gave rain, and the earth produced its fruit. Brethren, if anyone among you wanders from the truth, and someone turns him back, let him know that he who turns a sinner from the error of his way will save a soul from death and cover a multitude of sins.

Many people have questions about healing and the following questions are ones which are typically asked. If you find that your questions aren't among these being answered, just remember that you can go to the Lord and ask the Holy Spirit to teach you (John 14:26) and guide you into truth (John 16:13). God loves your questions because He has the answers for your life, and your story is going to be a powerful testimony. Be encouraged to go back to the lessons and listen to them again. Review your notes and meditate on God's Word. Use these questions and answers, and the video teachings, to receive and walk in healing. Then start stepping out in boldness and pointing out the things of the enemy that he's trying to do in other people's lives.

1. Does God test us with sickness?

2. I have been sick for so long, how can I change my vision for a future of health?

3. I say all the right words and I know I believe; why isn't it working?

4. If we are supposed to be healed and walk in this healing, are you saying we will never die?

Lesson 7
Faith for Healing

Instructor:
Daniel Amstutz

Note: All scriptures used in this lesson are quoted from the *New King James Version*.

I.   Fear works with physical symptoms, but on the other hand, faith works with the truth.

   A. If you're a believer, a follower of Jesus, you already have faith. That's the good news. You've got more than enough faith to be healed and to live life more abundantly, not less abundantly.

   B. Believing and faith are powerfully linked together. You can't believe without faith, but you can have faith and not believe.

   How then shall they call on Him in whom they have not believed? And how shall they believe in Him of whom they have not heard? And how shall they hear without a preacher? And how shall they preach unless they are sent? As it is written: "How beautiful are the feet of those who preach the gospel of peace, Who bring glad tidings of good things!" But they have not all obeyed the gospel. For Isaiah says, "Lord, who has believed our report?" So then faith comes by hearing, and hearing by the word of God.

   Romans 10:14–17

   C. We receive salvation through Jesus. We receive all that God has for us through Jesus, not through ourselves.

   Jesus said to him, "I am the way, the truth, and the life. No one comes to the Father except through Me."

   John 14:6

II. The Holy Spirit, His life, and His fruit in you include His download of faith into your redeemed spirit.

But the fruit of the Spirit is love, joy, peace, longsuffering, kindness, goodness, faithfulness, gentleness, self-control. Against such there is no law.

Galatians 5:22–23

A. We not only have faith, but we have the mind of Christ living in our spirit man.

For "who has known the mind of the LORD that he may instruct Him?" But we have the mind of Christ.

1 Corinthians 2:16

III. Faith comes by hearing and hearing by the Word of God. So, faith doesn't come down; it comes up so that it can come out.

So then faith comes by hearing, and hearing by the word of God.

Romans 10:17

A. What the Holy Ghost put in our spirit man is supernatural. The faith of God is nothing like natural faith.

B. What you have alive in you already is so far superior to anything that the world has to offer. Literally, it's priceless.

C. The things of the Spirit have to be spiritually discerned.

But the natural man does not receive the things of the Spirit of God, for they are foolishness to him; nor can he know them, because they are spiritually discerned.

1 Corinthians 2:14

D. You cannot separate faith from the Word of God. Faith comes through the revealed knowledge of God.

As His divine power has given to us all things that pertain to life and godliness, through the knowledge of Him who called us by glory and virtue, by which have been given to us exceedingly great and precious promises, that through these you may be partakers of the divine nature, having escaped the corruption that is in the world through lust.

2 Peter 1:3–4

IV. Faith will trust.

    A. We've never in Scripture been told to have faith in our faith. A lot of people don't put their faith in the Word of God, and they're not putting their faith in God—they're putting their faith in their faith.

So Jesus answered and said to them, "Have faith in God."

Mark 11:22

V. Hearing and healing are linked together.

    A. The people came to hear Him and be healed of their diseases.

And He came down with them and stood on a level place with a crowd of His disciples and a great multitude of people from all Judea and Jerusalem, and from the seacoast of Tyre and Sidon, who came to hear Him and be healed of their diseases.

Luke 6:17

    B. It's absolutely important to take heed, not only to what we hear, but to how we hear because how we hear will determine how we live.

Then He said to them, "Take heed what you hear. With the same measure you use, it will be measured to you; and to you who hear, more will be given.

Mark 4:24

    C. Faith comes by hearing, but so does fear.

VI. Faith works by love. In God's love is where we find supernatural hope.

Now hope does not disappoint, because the love of God has been poured out in our hearts by the Holy Spirit who was given to us.

Romans 5:5

    A. False hope can happen in the natural through well-meaning people, but it never comes from God. In God, and in the love of God, there is no such thing as false hope.

Hope deferred makes the heart sick, but when *the desire comes, it is a tree of life.*

Proverbs 13:12

B. Hope that is birthed in the love of God cannot be false hope.

C. This faith, hope, and love is Holy Ghost breathed. It is supernatural, alive and powerful, and able to change sickness into wellness. It's changing impossible into possible and negative reports into good reports.

D. Hope is like spiritual imagination. It paints the picture that your faith connects to. You meditate on that picture over, and over, and over until you become fully convinced.

E. We can call things that are not as though they are: why? Because we see a different picture on the inside of our hearts that will bring transformation from the inside to the outside.

(As it is written, "I have made you a father of many nations") in the presence of Him whom he believed—God, who gives life to the dead and calls those things which do not exist as though they did.

Romans 4:17

VII. Our faith doesn't create healing; it simply receives what God has already created. Even creating a miracle isn't the result of us creating something. God is the Creator, and He's the Healer, not us.

A. Abraham was a hundred years old, but God gave him a promise. In the natural, there was no hope, but God's Word contained the hope for that promise to be able to happen.

Who, contrary to hope, in hope believed, so that he became the father of many nations, according to what was spoken, "So shall your descendants be." And not being weak in faith, he did not consider his own body, already dead (since he was about a hundred years old), and the deadness of Sarah's womb.

Romans 4:18–19

B. Abraham became fully convinced, fully persuaded, that God was able to do what He had promised.

He did not waver at the promise of God through unbelief, but was strengthened in faith, giving glory to God, and being fully convinced that what He had promised He was also able to perform.

Romans 4:20–21

VIII. Don't check your body for the truth. Your body can only give you the facts, at best. Check the Word of God for truth. We need to look at things that are not seen.

While we do not look at the things which are seen, but at the things which are not seen. For the things which are seen are *temporary, but the things which are not seen* are *eternal.*

2 Corinthians 4:18

A. It takes no faith to believe the facts. It only takes faith to believe the truth.

And you shall know the truth, and the truth shall make you free.

John 8:32

B. If we're going to see the supernatural power and faith of God, which are already in us, come up from inside and actually make a difference in our lives, we've got to connect what we believe and how we're thinking to the Word of God.

C. This does not mean denying the facts. You need to face the facts but embrace the truth. That's the difference. We identify with the truth, with God's Word. We magnify the truth from the inside out and meditate in the truth day and night.

For we walk by faith, not by sight.

2 Corinthians 5:7

D. God's waiting for you to believe the report that He's already given you—the report that is a good report.

IX. Faith in the finished works of Jesus is the opposite of faith in your own works.

A. Jesus already took your sickness. He already took your disease. He already took your pain so that you don't have to.

B. Symptoms of sickness in your body don't have to be received and embraced as if they were true. Those lying symptoms are not the same thing as the truth. Jesus took your sickness. He took those symptoms. He knew you would never qualify for healing, so He did it on your behalf.

X. Faith doesn't create healing; faith receives healing because Jesus is the healer.

A. Faith can only receive what grace has provided through Jesus. His grace provided it all for us, but now faith can receive what Jesus has provided.

B. Any time we make ourselves the authors or the finishers, we're going to be disappointed with the results. Any time we make receiving about us, we will be disappointed.

C. Peter and John knew that this miracle was not about them. They knew it was the supernatural power of God flowing through them that made the difference in this man's life and actually changed his structure from being crippled to being made whole.

So when Peter saw it, he responded to the people: "Men of Israel, why do you marvel at this? Or why look so intently at us, as though by our own power or godliness we had made this man walk?

Acts 3:12

D. We don't receive through us; we receive through Jesus.

E. Put your faith in His name.

And His name, through faith in His name, has made this man strong, whom you see and know. Yes, the faith which comes through Him has given him this perfect sound-ness in the presence of you all.

Acts 3:16

F. God gets glory whenever people are healed. God is the one who gets glorified because Jesus is the one who did all the work.

XI. Faith is really all about, "I believe it and I receive it."

A. If you really believe what God's provided, and you really believe that your healing has been provided for by what Jesus did for you, then you know He already wants you to prosper and be in health.

Beloved, I pray that you may prosper in all things and be in health, just as your soul prospers.

3 John 1:2

B. It's not that we don't have faith; it's that we are marinated in unbelief and don't even know it.

Jesus said to him, "If you can believe, all things are possible to him who believes." Immediately the father of the child cried out and said with tears, "Lord, I believe; help my unbelief!"

Mark 9:23–24

C. When you're really in faith and believing God, there's a rest and peace in the midst of whatever is going on. It doesn't mean you're not ever going to be rattled or have opportunity to be discouraged, but there's will be a supernatural peace that will flow through your life as a result of what God has done.

D. When you believe you've already received it, you say, "Thank you," and you rest. You rest in the finished work of Jesus knowing that it's already been done.

But my heart stands in awe of Your word. I rejoice at Your word As one who finds great treasure.

Psalms 119:161–162

E. Our doubt doesn't change the truth, but the truth will change your doubt, your unbelief, and even your reality.

F. Faith will believe the promise instead of the problem.

G. The more we hear, the more we believe, and the more we renew our minds, the more we are transformed.

**LESSON REVIEW
QUESTIONS**

1. According to Romans 10:14–17, what is the link between believing and faith?

2. Why can't you separate faith from the Word of God?

3. Faith believes truth. Is a medical report truth? Explain your answer.

4. What will help you know if you are really in faith and believing God for your healing?

5. Explain the statement, "Healing is not about us, but it's for us."

6. What rating, from 0 (low) to 10 (high), would you give your faith for healing right now?

**LESSON REVIEW
ANSWERS**

1. According to Romans 10:14–17, what is the link between believing and faith?

   You can't believe without faith, but you can have faith and not believe.

2. Why can't you separate faith from the Word of God?

   Possible answers: Faith comes through the revealed knowledge of God; faith comes by hearing the Word of God.

3. Faith believes truth. Is a medical report truth? Explain your answer.

   Possible answer: A medical report might be a fact, but God's Word is the truth that trumps everything.

4. What will help you know if you are really in faith and believing God for your healing?

   If I am living in faith, I will have peace and joy.

5. Explain the statement, "Healing is not about us, but it's for us."

   Possible answer: Jesus did the work on the cross for me to be healed, but I benefit and receive the healing.

6. What rating, from 0 (low) to 10 (high), would you give your faith for healing right now?

   Answers will vary.

POINTS TO PONDER

- Fear is the opposite of faith, and fear is a terrible motivator. Fear is a tormenter. Fear will believe the facts or believe a lie, but it will receive both as if it were the truth, and that's the problem. It is faith in reverse.

- All of that Holy Ghost ability came to live in your spirit man the minute you were born again. You may not have known it, but it did. You've had faith alive in you ever since you were born again.

- When you know somebody loves you and has your best interest at heart, it's really easy to trust them. They build trust in your life through that love relationship. This is exactly what faith does with God and with the Word of God.

- If you're meditating and spending time on all the natural news of the world and wondering why you're not seeing victory in your life, think—what are you listening to?

- God's got a good report for you. We've got to be listening to the Word of God because that's where our faith is going to come from. So, if you're listening to things contrary to the Word of God, you're not going to have faith for healing. Faith is so important to the heart of God that without faith it is impossible to please Him.

- In the love of God is where we find hope, and this kind of hope cannot disappoint.

- God is God. His Word is true, and what He's given us is something completely supernatural that can cause the impossible to become possible for you right now.

- Many people think that facts and truth are the same thing. No, God's Word is the truth, and truth will always trump your reality.

- Let the Word be magnified in your life, not the circumstances.

- The medical report may be factual, but the Word of God has the supernatural power to actually change those facts, to actually change the reality of what you've known into something brand new.

- When your faith is in Jesus and His finished works, then it can't be about you and your works.

- Healing is not about us, but it's for us.

- When people supernaturally receive the provision that the Lord has already provided, the glory goes to God.

- When you go to see a doctor, they will do their best to give you a diagnosis, but it may or not be a good report. On the other hand, God's got a good report for you with your name on it.

- There is a joy and peace in believing that will be your strength, even in the midst of challenges. You've got the fruit of the Holy Ghost living on the inside of you as you believe God in the midst of all that's going on around you.

- We make it hard when we make it about ourselves. But when we're truly in faith, we're in a place of rest, as if we have found great treasure, and the joy that comes from it is literally our strength.

- God's Word is truth, and when we know His Word, we're set free from doubt, from unbelief, and from limitation.

- Faith believes God's Word and values it like treasure.

GO DEEPER

Self-Examination Questions

Do you identify with the hope the world gives or with the hope that the Word gives? Why?

Are you fully persuaded that God is able to do what He promised in His Word that He would do?

If you were to receive what you've been believing or doubting for right now, what would happen in your body? Is that what you would want to happen? If not, what can you do to change your thoughts?

Prayer Points

Use these prayer points to write and to pray your own powerful prayer:

- Thank God that He sent His Word.
- Thank God that you have faith.
- Praise God that you already have faith because you're born again.
- Declare that fear has no place in you.
- Proclaim that your faith trusts in God and receives what Jesus did on the cross.
- Thank God for supernatural hope.
- Call things that are not as though they are.
- Praise God that He is THE healer.
- Thank God that His Word is truth and your faith believes the truth.
- Thank God that He has a good report for you.
- Praise God that healing is for you.

Action Steps

- In your Healing University journal, write down an exhaustive list of statements about faith from this lesson. Rewatch the video again and make your list. Ponder and come up with other statements that you can write down. Match verses from the lesson to each statement. Search the Bible for more verses to add to the list. Choose at least two verses to commit to memory this week.

- Settle in your heart that faith believes the Word of God, receives the truth, and takes ahold of it. Examine your heart and, when you are ready, make the following declaration and don't waver from it:

  I believe that my faith doesn't create my healing, but by faith I receive my healing because Jesus is the healer.

  _____ (sign and date)

- Write your own answer to this question: *How will you get faith for your healing?*

SCRIPTURES

Faith for Healing

Luke 8:49–50

While He was still speaking, someone came from the ruler of the synagogue's house, saying to him, "Your daughter is dead. Do not trouble the Teacher." But when Jesus heard it, He answered him, saying, "Do not be afraid; only believe, and she will be made well."

Romans 10:14–17

How then shall they call on Him in whom they have not believed? And how shall they believe in Him of whom they have not heard? And how shall they hear without a preacher? And how shall they preach unless they are sent? As it is written: "How beautiful are the feet of those who preach the gospel of peace, Who bring glad tidings of good things!" But they have not all obeyed the gospel. For Isaiah says, "Lord, who has believed our report?" So then faith comes by hearing, and hearing by the word of God.

2 Corinthians 5:17

Therefore, if anyone is in Christ, he is a new creation; old things have passed away; behold, all things have become new.

John 14:6

Jesus said to him, "I am the way, the truth, and the life. No one comes to the Father except through Me."

Galatians 5:22–23

But the fruit of the Spirit is love, joy, peace, longsuffering, kindness, goodness, faithfulness, gentleness, self-control. Against such there is no law.

1 Corinthians 2:16

For "who has known the mind of the Lord that he may instruct Him?" But we have the mind of Christ.

John 14:27

Peace I leave with you, My peace I give to you; not as the world gives do I give to you. Let not your heart be troubled, neither let it be afraid.

1 Corinthians 2:14

But the natural man does not receive the things of the Spirit of God, for they are foolishness to him; nor can he know them, *because they are spiritually discerned.*

Mark 9:23–25

Jesus said to him, "If you can believe, all things are *possible to him who believes." Immediately the father of the child cried out and said with tears, "Lord, I believe; help my unbelief!" When Jesus saw that the people came running together, He rebuked the unclean spirit, saying to it, "Deaf and dumb spirit, I command you, come out of him and enter him no more!"*

Romans 10:8

But what does it say? "The word is near you, in your mouth and in your heart"(that is, the word of faith which we preach).

2 Peter 1:3–4

As His divine power has given to us all things that pertain *to life and godliness, through the knowledge of Him who called us by glory and virtue, by which have been given to us exceedingly great and precious promises, that through these you may be partakers of the divine nature, having escaped the corruption* that is *in the world through lust.*

Romans 12:3

For I say, through the grace given to me, to everyone who is among you, not to think of himself *more highly than he ought to think, but to think soberly, as God has dealt to each one a measure of faith.*

Ephesians 2:8

For by grace you have been saved through faith, and that not of yourselves; it is *the gift of God*

Mark 11:22

So Jesus answered and said to them, "Have faith in God."

Luke 6:17

> *And He came down with them and stood on a level place with a crowd of His disciples and a great multitude of people from all Judea and Jerusalem, and from the seacoast of Tyre and Sidon, who came to hear Him and be healed of their diseases.*

Mark 4:24

> *Then He said to them, "Take heed what you hear. With the same measure you use, it will be measured to you; and to you who hear, more will be given.*

Luke 8:18

> *Therefore take heed how you hear. For whoever has, to him more will be given; and whoever does not have, even what he seems to have will be taken from him."*

Hebrews 11:6

> *But without faith it is impossible to please Him, for he who comes to God must believe that He is, and that He is a rewarder of those who diligently seek Him.*

Hebrews 11:1

> *Now faith is the substance of things hoped for, the evidence of things not seen.*

Galatians 5:6

> *For in Christ Jesus neither circumcision nor uncircumcision avails anything, but faith working through love.*

Romans 5:5

> *Now hope does not disappoint, because the love of God has been poured out in our hearts by the Holy Spirit who was given to us.*

Proverbs 13:12

> *Hope deferred makes the heart sick, but when the desire comes, it is a tree of life.*

Romans 4:17

> *(As it is written, "I have made you a father of many nations") in the presence of Him whom he believed—God, who gives life to the dead and calls those things which do not exist as though they did.*

Romans 4:18-19

Who, contrary to hope, in hope believed, so that he became the father of many nations, according to what was spoken, "So shall your descendants be." And not being weak in faith, he did not consider his own body, already dead (since he was about a hundred years old), and the deadness of Sarah's womb.

Romans 4:20-21

He did not waver at the promise of God through unbelief, but was strengthened in faith, giving glory to God, and being fully convinced that what He had promised He was also able to perform.

2 Corinthians 4:18

While we do not look at the things which are seen, but at the things which are not seen. For the things which are seen are temporary, but the things which are not seen are eternal.

John 17:17

Sanctify them by Your truth. Your word is truth.

John 8:32

And you shall know the truth, and the truth shall make you free.

2 Corinthians 5:7

For we walk by faith, not by sight.

Acts 3:1-10

Now Peter and John went up together to the temple at the hour of prayer, the ninth hour. And a certain man lame from his mother's womb was carried, whom they laid daily at the gate of the temple which is called Beautiful, to ask alms from those who entered the temple; who, seeing Peter and John about to go into the temple, asked for alms. And fixing his eyes on him, with John, Peter said, "Look at us." So he gave them his attention, expecting to receive something from them. Then Peter said, "Silver and gold I do not have, but what I do have I give you: In the name of Jesus Christ of Nazareth, rise up and walk." And he took him by the right hand and lifted him up, and immediately his feet and ankle bones received strength. So he, leaping up, stood and walked and entered the temple with them—walking, leaping, and praising God. And all the people saw him walking and praising God. Then they knew that it was he who sat begging alms at the Beautiful Gate of the temple; and they were filled with wonder and amazement at what had happened to him.

Acts 4:22

For the man was over forty years old on whom this miracle of healing had been performed.

Acts 3:12

So when Peter saw it, he responded to the people: "Men of Israel, why do you marvel at this? Or why look so intently at us, as though by our own power or godliness we had made this man walk?

Colossians 1:27

To them God willed to make known what are the riches of the glory of this mystery among the Gentiles: which is Christ in you, the hope of glory.

Acts 3:16

And His name, through faith in His name, has made this man strong, whom you see and know. Yes, the faith which comes through Him has given him this perfect soundness in the presence of you all.

Philippians 2:9

Therefore God also has highly exalted Him and given Him the name which is above every name.

3 John 1:2

Beloved, I pray that you may prosper in all things and be in health, just as your soul prospers.

Isaiah 53:1

Who has believed our report? And to whom has the arm of the LORD been revealed?

Psalms 119:161–162

Princes persecute me without a cause, But my heart stands in awe of Your word. I rejoice at Your word As one who finds great treasure.

Mark 16:17–18

And these signs will follow those who believe: In My name they will cast out demons; they will speak with new tongues; they will take up serpents; and if they drink anything deadly, it will by no means hurt them; they will lay hands on the sick, and they will recover.

Matthew 9:28–30

And when He had come into the house, the blind men came to Him. And Jesus said to them, "Do you believe that I am able to do this?" They said to Him, "Yes, Lord." Then He touched their eyes, saying, "According to your faith let it be to you." And their eyes were opened. And Jesus sternly warned them, saying, "See that no one knows it."

Lesson 8
Wisdom for Living in Health and Healing

Instructor:
Duane Sheriff

Note: All scriptures used in this lesson are quoted from the *New King James Version*.

I.   If we're going to walk in healing, then we have to understand the kingdom of God. We have to have wisdom not only to be healed, but also to maintain that healing and walk in the light of that healing.

   A. Just because we receive a healing doesn't necessarily mean we can maintain it. Just like many people who have received the forgiveness of their sins wind up back in a sin again, some people who have received a healing struggle with that same sickness or disease again. It doesn't mean they weren't healed any more than it means believers who still struggle with sin weren't cleansed and washed of that sin.

   B. Just because we're healed of something doesn't mean we're not subject to sickness or disease again because we live in a fallen world.

   C. We have to have knowledge of certain things that are violating kingdom principles, or spiritual laws and creating problems in our lives.

   My people are destroyed for lack of knowledge. Because you have rejected knowledge,
   I also will reject you from being priest for Me; Because you have forgotten the law of
   your God, I also will forget your children.

   Hosea 4:6

II.   Wisdom is vital, and we can't have wisdom without the Word of God.

   A. If you want to know truth in regard to God's plan for your life, go to the Word.

   Sanctify them by Your truth. Your word is truth.

   John 17:17

B. Jesus has brought wisdom to us, and we need to access that wisdom by faith and by diligently searching the Scriptures and knowing the truth.

But of Him you are in Christ Jesus, who became for us wisdom from God—and righteousness and sanctification and redemption.

1 Corinthians 1:30

C. If you continue in God's Word, you'll have wisdom and understanding that will make you free from sin, sickness, disease, oppression, and depression.

D. God wants for you to have the eyes of your understanding opened and enlightened and for you to know His heartbeat, His love for you, and His truth in a way that makes you free.

III. Prosperity and health are connected to the prosperity of your soul.

Beloved, I pray that you may prosper in all things and be in health, just as your soul prospers.

3 John 2

A. It is a top priority that you prosper, and prosperity is not limited to just finances.

B. Many people want to be healed, but they don't want to renew their minds to the Word of God.

And do not be conformed to this world, but be transformed by the renewing of your mind, that you may prove what is that good and acceptable and perfect will of God.

Romans 12:2

C. The Word and the wisdom of God sets you free from unforgiveness, bitterness, wrath, anger, and strife. These things in people's hearts open them up to being unhealthy.

For I rejoiced greatly when brethren came and testified of the truth that is in you, just as you walk in the truth.

3 John 3

D. What pleases God is the Word of God working in your heart and in your life.

I have no greater joy than to hear that my children walk in truth.

3 John 4

IV. Faith begins and ends where a knowledge of God's Word is acquired.

   A. God's Word is what changes us; God's Word is what cleanses us; God's Word is what brings faith to receive His goodness in our lives.

V. One of the primary things that a lot of Christians miss is forgiving other people and understanding the wisdom connected with forgiveness.

   A. The church and Paul invoked a form of church discipline on someone who was living in immorality and not willing to deal with it. He repented, and Paul encouraged the Christians to confirm their love for him, to embrace him, to forgive him, and to have compassion on him.

   For to this end I also wrote, that I might put you to the test, whether you are obedient in all things.

   2 Corinthians 2:9

   B. Unforgiveness is a device that Satan uses to steal, kill, and destroy.

   Now whom you forgive anything, I also forgive. For if indeed I have forgiven anything, I have forgiven that one for your sakes in the presence of Christ, lest Satan should take advantage of us; for we are not ignorant of his devices.

   2 Corinthians 2:10–11

   C. Christians today are deceived.

   Do not be deceived, God is not mocked; for whatever a man sows, that he will also reap. For he who sows to his flesh will of the flesh reap corruption, but he who sows to the Spirit will of the Spirit reap everlasting life.

   Galatians 6:7–8

   D. God loves you. God doesn't punish you. God doesn't turn on you if you commit a sin. However, sin is deadly and dangerous, and it opens the door for Satan.

The thief does not come except to steal, and to kill, and to destroy. I have come that they may have life, and that they may have it more abundantly.

John 10:10

E. Satan can steal the healing that Jesus has provided for you in His amazing grace if you choose not to forgive.

F. One of the things that helps you forgive anybody of anything is to turn them over to God. God is a just and righteous God. Vengeance is His, and He will repay.

Beloved, do not avenge yourselves, but rather *give place to wrath; for it is written, "Vengeance is Mine, I will repay," says the Lord.*

Romans 12:19

G. There's a difference between forgiving and trusting. There are people I have forgiven who have wronged me deeply, but I don't trust them. I have forgiven them, but wisdom says not to trust them.

VI. We need to avoid the wisdom of man and embrace the wisdom of God.

Who is wise and understanding among you? Let him show by good conduct that his works are done in the meekness of wisdom. But if you have bitter envy and self-seeking in your hearts, do not boast and lie against the truth. This wisdom does not descend from above, but is earthly, sensual, demonic. For where envy and self-seeking exist, confusion and every evil thing are there. But the wisdom that is from above is first pure, then peaceable, gentle, willing to yield, full of mercy and good fruits, without partiality and without hypocrisy. Now the fruit of righteousness is sown in peace by those who make peace.

James 3:13–18

A. The wisdom of this world is earthly wisdom. It is sensual (of the five senses) and demonic.

B. Strife is division, discord, unforgiveness, and a form of offense. The devil comes in when there is strife, bitterness, and anger in our hearts and brings every evil work. Sickness and disease are evil works.

C. Wisdom sows God's will and love in peace, not in anger, wrath, bitterness, self-seeking, or envy.

D. When you hang on to resentment, it damages you on the inside. God wants you to repent and release it.

For as he thinks in his heart, so is he. "Eat and drink!" he says to you, But his heart is not with you.

Proverbs 23:7

E. We have to be a people of forgiveness. We have to see how much God has forgiven us of all of our sins and be quick to forgive others.

Pursue peace with all people, and holiness, without which no one will see the Lord: looking carefully lest anyone fall short of the grace of God; lest any root of bitterness springing up cause trouble, and by this many become defiled.

Hebrews 12:14–15

F. Any time we're hurt, hurt's not the real issue between us and God and people. Unforgiveness is the issue.

G. Embrace grace, because you are falling short of grace when you are in unforgiveness.

VII. The way to bind the devil is to repent of unforgiveness.

A. I bind the devil by forgiving people because he wants to use unforgiveness as a device against me, and I am wiser than the devil.

B. When you confess, Satan can't hold that over you anymore.

If we confess our sins, He is faithful and just to forgive us our sins and to cleanse us from all unrighteousness.

1 John 1:9

C. God's not holding anything over us, but the devil will.

D. Be quick to repent and quick to forgive, and watch the health of God spring forth in your heart and in your body.

LESSON REVIEW QUESTIONS

1. What does it mean if a healed person feels sick again?

2. How does Hosea 4:6 relate to a healed Christian's confusion about a sickness returning?

3. According to 3 John 4, what brings God the greatest joy?

4. Describe characteristics of God's wisdom and of the world's wisdom.

5. As you walk in God's wisdom, what will you see in your life?

6. How does unforgiveness affect a Christian?

7. How does repentance affect a Christian?

**LESSON REVIEW
ANSWERS**

1. What does it mean if a healed person feels sick again?

   Possible answers: A healed person can feel sick again because we live in a fallen world; the person might not have God's Word in them or know how to resist the sickness; there might be unforgiveness that has opened the door to sickness.

2. How does Hosea 4:6 relate to a healed Christian's confusion about a sickness returning?

   Hosea 4:6 points out that God's people are destroyed from a lack of knowledge. Christians need to know what God's Word says and apply that wisdom to their lives so they can walk in health and help others.

3. According to 3 John 4, what brings God the greatest joy?

   God's greatest joy is when His children walk in truth.

4. Describe characteristics of God's wisdom and of the world's wisdom.
   Possible answers: God's wisdom is accessed by faith, it brings peace, renews our minds, makes us free, and should be embraced and followed.

   The world's wisdom is sensual, of the five senses, demonic, and should be avoided.

5. As you walk in God's wisdom, what will you see in your life?

   There will be a faith in God's grace that will cause a channel of His blessings to begin to manifest on a regular basis in my life, and I will have peace.

6. How does unforgiveness affect a Christian?

   Unforgiveness opens a door for Satan to steal, kill, and destroy, and it damages us inside and holds us captive.

7. How does repentance affect a Christian?

   Repentance binds Satan and releases God's forgiveness, which cleanses our souls.

POINTS TO PONDER

- Sin and sickness are all around us; we're all being tempted to sin and we're all being tempted with sickness. We have to resist sickness just like we have learned to resist sin.

- God doesn't just will to heal, He wills to heal everybody all the time and for us to be healthy. He wills for us to be whole.

- God wants us to understand healing and have wisdom so that we can minister the grace of God to other people.

- We live in a very arrogant, high-minded, intellectual culture. People think they are so smart, and they think they're so wise, yet they not only live in sin that brings death into their lives, they even celebrate it.

- The good, acceptable, and perfect will of God is that you not only be healed, but also walk in health and become a channel of God's healing into other's lives.

- As you walk in the Word, which is God's wisdom for your life, faith in God's grace will cause a channel of His blessings to begin to manifest on a regular basis in your life.

- If you're going to walk in health, you need God's Word. You need God's wisdom.

- One of the primary things that creates havoc in people's lives is letting unforgiveness and offense get into their hearts and lives. The Scriptures are clear on how important it is that believers be people of forgiveness.

- We're broken, and we're hurt. If we don't know how to get healed of that hurt, it can turn into bitterness, wrath, strife, and division.

- Forgiveness is a choice. Unforgiveness is also a choice, and it yields power to Satan.

- If we embrace unforgiveness, we open the door for every evil work, including sickness and disease.

- We weren't designed by God to carry offense and unforgiveness in our hearts. When we do, it affects our health.

- Many people are all messed up, and they blame other people instead of realizing their own unforgiveness has opened the door for the devil to steal, kill, and destroy.

- Forgiveness is a choice, not an emotion. It doesn't mean you forget, and it doesn't mean you ever have to trust them again. You release them to God, and pursue peace.

- Everybody's not at peace with me, but I'm at peace with everybody.

- When somebody mistreats me and I struggle to forgive them, I know it's the devil trying to get me to choose not to forgive, so he can steal, kill, and destroy. So, I bind the devil and I forgive them.

- When I repent and receive the faithfulness and justice of God to forgive me, He washes and cleanses me of all unrighteousness. Now the effect of that unforgiveness is washed and cleansed. Bitterness cannot take root.

- Walk in God's wisdom and Word. Be a student of the Word of God and His wisdom. Be quick to repent. Be quick to forgive. Be quick to let offenses go.

GO DEEPER

Self-Examination Questions

Do you really believe God wants you to prosper and be in health?

On a scale from 1–10 (low to high), how willing are you to commit to walking in the wisdom that you are learning?

Based on today's lesson, are there areas of unforgiveness and strife that are robbing you of health? What will you do about those areas?

Prayer Points

Use these prayer points to write and to pray your own powerful prayer:

- Praise God that His wisdom will cause you to walk in healing.
- Ask God to reveal to you exactly who you need to forgive.
- Repent of any sin, especially sins of anger, strife, bitterness, unforgiveness, and offense.
- Thank God that He cleanses you and washes you from all unrighteousness.
- Offer forgiveness to each person that God brings to your mind.
- Thank God that repentance binds Satan.
- Declare that Satan has no place in your life and can no longer rob you of your health.
- Praise God for the peace that following His wisdom brings to your life.
- Thank God for the wisdom that you are gaining that will help others to also be set free.

Action Steps

- In your Healing University journal, create a visual representation of yourself as the "gardener of your heart" in regard to the wisdom of God leading to the uprooting of unwanted crops of unforgiveness and strife. Draw and label a picture showing each hurt that is a seed planted in your heart that needs to be weeded out through forgiveness. Show seeds that you allowed to grow due to offense and unforgiveness and the effects they have on you and your health. Imagine your prayer of confession of that unforgiveness acts as weed killer. Apply the weed killer to keep the seed of offense and unforgiveness from continuing to grow and rob you of your health. Do not let the seed remain where it can reopen that hurt in you. Depict the removal of that seed from the garden of your heart and plant peace and joy in its place.

- Settle in your heart that God's will isn't just to heal you, but also that you walk in health. God's wisdom shows you how to walk in health. Examine your heart and, when you are ready, make the following declaration and don't waver from it:

I believe God wants me well and wants me to walk in health. I choose to apply God's wisdom to my life, and I choose to forgive so that health will spring up in me.

_____ (sign and date)

- Write your own answer to this question: *How will you use God's wisdom to gain and keep your healing?*

Wisdom for Living in Health and Healing

Hosea 4:6

> *My people are destroyed for lack of knowledge. Because you have rejected knowledge, I also will reject you from being priest for Me; Because you have forgotten the law of your God, I also will forget your children.*

John 17:17

> *Sanctify them by Your truth. Your word is truth.*

1 Corinthians 1:30

> *But of Him you are in Christ Jesus, who became for us wisdom from God—and righteousness and sanctification and redemption.*

John 8:31–32

> *Then Jesus said to those Jews who believed Him, "If you abide in My word, you are My disciples indeed. And you shall know the truth, and the truth shall make you free."*

3 John 2

> *Beloved, I pray that you may prosper in all things and be in health, just as your soul prospers.*

Romans 12:2

> *And do not be conformed to this world, but be transformed by the renewing of your mind, that you may prove what is that good and acceptable and perfect will of God.*

3 John 3–4

> *For I rejoiced greatly when brethren came and testified of the truth that is in you, just as you walk in the truth. I have no greater joy than to hear that my children walk in truth.*

Romans 10:17

So then faith comes by hearing, and hearing by the word of God.

2 Corinthians 2:9

For to this end I also wrote, that I might put you to the test, whether you are obedient in all things.

2 Corinthians 2:10–11

Now whom you forgive anything, I also forgive. For if indeed I have forgiven anything, I have forgiven that one for your sakes in the presence of Christ, lest Satan should take advantage of us; for we are not ignorant of his devices.

Galatians 6:7–8

Do not be deceived, God is not mocked; for whatever a man sows, that he will also reap. For he who sows to his flesh will of the flesh reap corruption, but he who sows to the Spirit will of the Spirit reap everlasting life.

John 10:10

The thief does not come except to steal, and to kill, and to destroy. I have come that they may have life, and that they may have it more abundantly.

Hebrews 13:5

Let your conduct be without covetousness; be content with such things as you have. For He Himself has said, "I will never leave you nor forsake you."

Galatians 3:13

Christ has redeemed us from the curse of the law, having become a curse for us (for it is written, "Cursed is everyone who hangs on a tree").

Matthew 10:16

Behold, I send you out as sheep in the midst of wolves. Therefore be wise as serpents and harmless as doves.

James 3:13–18

Who is wise and understanding among you? Let him show by good conduct that his works are done in the meekness of wisdom. But if you have bitter envy and self-

seeking in your hearts, do not boast and lie against the truth. This wisdom does not descend from above, but is earthly, sensual, demonic. For where envy and self-seeking exist, confusion and every evil thing are *there. But the wisdom that is from above is first pure, then peaceable, gentle, willing to yield, full of mercy and good fruits, without partiality and without hypocrisy. Now the fruit of righteousness is sown in peace by those who make peace.*

Romans 12:19

Beloved, do not avenge yourselves, but rather *give place to wrath; for it is written, "Vengeance* is *Mine, I will repay," says the Lord.*

Proverbs 14:30

A sound heart is *life to the body, but envy* is *rottenness to the bones.*

Proverbs 23:7

For as he thinks in his heart, so is *he. "Eat and drink!" he says to you, but his heart is not with you.*

Hebrews 12:14–15

Pursue peace with all people, *and holiness, without which no one will see the Lord: looking carefully lest anyone fall short of the grace of God; lest any root of bitterness springing up cause trouble, and by this many become defiled.*

Romans 12:18

If it is possible, as much as depends on you, live peaceably with all men.

Hebrews 12:15

Looking carefully lest anyone fall short of the grace of God; lest any root of bitterness springing up cause trouble, and by this many become defiled.

1 John 1:9

If we confess our sins, He is faithful and just to forgive us our *sins and to cleanse us from all unrighteousness.*

1 John 1:7

But if we walk in the light as He is in the light, we have fellowship with one another, and the blood of Jesus Christ His Son cleanses us from all sin.

Proverbs 24:16

For a righteous man *may fall seven times And rise again, But the wicked shall fall by calamity.*

Proverbs 13:10

By pride comes nothing but strife, But with the well-advised is *wisdom.*

Lesson 9
Mental Health
Instructor:
Carlie Terradez

Note: All scriptures used in this lesson are quoted from the *New King James Version*.

I.   What we think in our hearts affects who we become, how we act, what we say, what we experience, and how we feel. It affects our health.

For as he thinks in his heart, so is he. "Eat and drink!" he says to you, But his heart is not with you.

Proverbs 23:7

A. Health is linked to mental prosperity. Health is linked to our soul prospering. As we start to think healthy, we'll start to be healthy.

Beloved, I pray that you may prosper in all things and be in health, just as your soul prospers.

3 John 2

B. If we are constantly speaking out negative words, we'll see the fruit of those words in our flesh. It'll affect our health. Negative words come from negative thinking.

Brood of vipers! How can you, being evil, speak good things? For out of the abundance of the heart the mouth speaks.

Matthew 12:34

II. If we want to change what we see on the outside, we have to first take a look at what we're seeing on the inside.

I beseech you therefore, brethren, by the mercies of God, that you present your bodies a living sacrifice, holy, acceptable to God, which is your reasonable service. And do not be conformed to this world, but be transformed by the renewing of your mind, that you may prove what is that good and acceptable and perfect will of God.

Romans 12:1–2

A. When we go through renewing our mind to the Word of God, it's not necessarily a comfortable experience.

B. There is a growth process when we go through that metamorphosis.

C. We need to take a long hard look at ourselves and examine what's in our hearts. When we are mentally healthy and have our opinions and our belief systems formed by the Word of God, we're going to have Word of God results. Mental health and physical health are intrinsically linked.

D. The fear of sickness will motivate people to reach for healing. Unfortunately, fear will only take people so far. It is a horrible motivator. Fear is the opposite of faith.

For God has not given us a spirit of fear, but of power and of love and of a sound mind.

2 Timothy 1:7

III. There are many influences in the world today. They come to choke the Word and stop it from becoming fruitful. We get distracted by living in a busy world.

And the cares of this world, the deceitfulness of riches, and the desires for other things entering in choke the word, and it becomes unfruitful.

Mark 4:19

A. If we're not careful, our ways and our thought processes will be more influenced by the world than by the Word of God.

B. Doubts come from the heart. Faith will overshadow doubt in our hearts when we release it. When we speak words of faith, they will crush thoughts of unbelief.

So Jesus answered and said to them, "Have faith in God. For assuredly, I say to you, whoever says to this mountain, 'Be removed and be cast into the sea,' and does not doubt in his heart, but believes that those things he says will be done, he will have whatever he says.

Mark 11:22–23

IV. We can actually change what we are thinking by changing what we are speaking.

   A. The only way to remove a lie, a negative thought system, or a wrong belief is to replace it with the truth.

   B. If we want to experience mental freedom—that means freedom from depression, anxiety, fear, worry, distress, and confusion—we need to start speaking the Word of God over our lives.

   C. If we want to find our purpose, we need to make sure that we are speaking the Word of God over our lives. We can actually guide our hearts.

   D. Our feelings follow our thoughts. What we're thinking upon produces feelings and physical responses. If we entertain thoughts for long, what we think on produces feelings. When we entertain those feelings, we'll start to act out what we feel.

   E. We cannot expect to walk in health and healing without first changing our thinking.

V. Fear and mental anguish are bondage. We entangle ourselves with a yoke of bondage. Having once become free, we can step back into bondage if our minds are not renewed and if our old patterns of thinking have not been changed.

   Stand fast therefore in the liberty by which Christ has made us free, and do not be entangled again with a yoke of bondage.

                                                                    Galatians 5:1

   A. It's what we meditate on that matters, and our job is to stop negative thoughts from landing.

   For though we walk in the flesh, we do not war according to the flesh. For the weapons of our warfare are not carnal but mighty in God for pulling down strongholds, casting down arguments and every high thing that exalts itself against the knowledge of God, bringing every thought into captivity to the obedience of Christ, and being ready to punish all disobedience when your obedience is fulfilled.

                                                                    2 Corinthians 10:3–6

   B. Abundant life comes from renewing your mind to the Word of God. Word of God results come from Word of God thinking.

C. If we want to pull down the strongholds in our lives once and for all, and be mentally healthy, there's only one way to do it effectively—through God.

D. Measure thoughts by the John 10:10 rule. If those thoughts are coming to kill, to steal, or destroy, then they're not good and they're not from God.

The thief does not come except to steal, and to kill, and to destroy. I have come that they may have life, and that they may have it more abundantly.

John 10:10

E. If we want to see transformation in our lives, we cannot be passive and neglect our mental health.

F. The devil will use fear to keep you in bondage. That is the yoke of bondage for which Christ has set you free. But if we do not renew our minds and have our opinions of ourselves, and our futures, determined by the Word of God, they will be determined by something else. We'll find ourselves slipping back into that yoke of bondage, slipping back into fear.

Inasmuch then as the children have partaken of flesh and blood, He Himself likewise shared in the same, that through death He might destroy him who had the power of death, that is, the devil, and release those who through fear of death were all their lifetime subject to bondage.

Hebrews 2:14–15

G. We have to decide to get the Word of God out and use it like a weapon against the thoughts of the enemy when those thoughts come.

VI. Peace is the antidote to fear.

You will keep him in perfect peace, Whose mind is stayed on You, Because he trusts in You.

Isaiah 26:3

A. We're not trying to get something from God that we haven't already got. One of the fruits of the Spirit is peace. We have received the Prince of Peace. He's the antidote to fear.

But the fruit of the Spirit is love, joy, peace, longsuffering, kindness, goodness, faith-fulness, gentleness, self-control. Against such there is no law.

Galatians 5:22–23

VII. We need to break patterns of wrong thinking and renew our minds to what the Word of God says.

A. We need to spot where wrong thinking has become a stronghold. How do we do that? The Holy Spirit is our helper.

B. If we need peace in our lives, one way to renew our minds is to respond in faith.

Be anxious for nothing, but in everything by prayer and supplication, with thanksgiving, let your requests be made known to God; and the peace of God, which surpasses all understanding, will guard your hearts and minds through Christ Jesus. Finally, brethren, whatever things are true, whatever things are noble, whatever things are just, whatever things are pure, whatever things are lovely, whatever things are of good report, if there is any virtue and if there is anything praiseworthy—meditate on these things. The things which you learned and received and heard and saw in me, these do, and the God of peace will be with you.

Philippians 4:6–9

C. Keep the Word of God before you day and night. Meditate on these things, and they will make your way prosperous.

This Book of the Law shall not depart from your mouth, but you shall meditate in it day and night, that you may observe to do according to all that is written in it. For then you will make your way prosperous, and then you will have good success. Have I not commanded you? Be strong and of good courage; do not be afraid, nor be dismayed, for the LORD your God is with you wherever you go."

Joshua 1:8–9

D. The power of the spoken Word of God over your life is life-transforming. The words of our mouths will alter the doubts; they'll crush the doubts that arise in our hearts. When the Word of God comes out of our mouths, God rejoices.

My son, if your heart is wise, My heart will rejoice—indeed, I myself; Yes, my inmost being will rejoice When your lips speak right things.

Hear, my son, and be wise; And guide your heart in the way.

Proverbs 23:15–16 and 19

E. If we want to advance in life in a healthy, productive way, if we want to see progress in something, we need to be calling our lives blessed.

F. If you don't know what to think, just speak the Word of God. You can't go wrong with the truth of the Word. The Word of God is so powerful, even unbelievers will start responding to it.

G. A heart that's left unprotected is a heart that has been left without leadership. We need to be leading our hearts, guiding our own hearts.

H. Speak the desired end result of your life, of your kids, of your body, of your situations.

I. Follow the pattern of sound teaching, which you have heard.

Hold fast the pattern of sound words which you have heard from me, in faith and love which are in Christ Jesus. That good thing which was committed to you, keep by the Holy Spirit who dwells in us.

2 Timothy 1:13–14

J. Take the Word of God. Take the treasure and use it to guard your heart and mind in Christ Jesus.

LESSON REVIEW QUESTIONS

1. If you hear yourself speaking negative words, what is the source?

2. Should Christians wonder if God wants them to have mental prosperity? Explain your answer.

3. What advice does Romans 12:1–2 offer to help a person change?

4. What role can the Word of God play in someone's mental health?

5. How does fear affect mental health?

6. Is it enough to just read God's Word if we want to have prosperous mental health?

7. What scripture from today's lesson will you meditate on for your mental health and why?

1. If you hear yourself speaking negative words, what is the source?

   If you speak negatively, you are thinking negative thoughts, and they are in your heart. Your mouth speaks what is in your heart.

2. Should Christians wonder if God wants them to have mental prosperity? Explain your answer.

   No; God wants us to prosper in all areas as our souls prosper. He wants us healthy, and part of being healthy is mental prosperity.

3. What advice does Romans 12:1–2 offer to help a person change?

   Romans 12:1–2 tells us not to conform to this world but to renew our minds.

4. What role can the Word of God play in someone's mental health?

   Possible answers: The Word of God can guide a person to renew their thoughts and cast out thoughts of fear; Scripture can be meditated on and used to replace lies and negative thoughts; the Word of God is a weapon to use against the enemy and the strongholds in our minds.

5. How does fear affect mental health?

   Fear brings mental bondage and is the opposite of faith. Negative thoughts can lead to fear. Fear can lead to physical problems.

6. Is it enough to just read God's Word if we want to have prosperous mental health?

   No; Reading God's Word is wonderful, but speaking out the Word helps us take ownership of it.

7. What scripture from today's lesson will you meditate on for your mental health, and why?

   Answers will vary.

POINTS TO PONDER

- Healing always manifests in our thinking first. As we think in our hearts, so we become. If we think like an unhealthy person, have negative mindsets, or constantly speak out toxic words, we will have those results. Our words have power.

- The business world, the marketing world, and the television industry all understand the power of words.

- What's in your heart will eventually come out of your mouth. So, if you don't like what's coming out of your mouth, find out what's in your heart.

- Sometimes we'll find that our actions and our belief systems are not based upon the Word of God but upon something else. That is why we aren't getting the kind of results that we want.

- If you've got dysfunction in your life in some area, then there needs to be a metamorphosis in your thinking.

- We cannot approach healing in fear and expect to receive. We approach the Healer in faith and expect to receive.

- The way to crush doubts in your heart is to start speaking what the Word of God says about your situation.

- As you start speaking the Word of God over your life, you will have whatever you say. You will start to crush any doubts that start to arise or try to surface in your heart.

- Whatever is a problem for you and needs renewing in your mind, there's a scripture you can stand on it for it.

- If I go into your garden and I see cucumber plants growing, I don't need to have been there when you planted to know what kind of seeds you planted. If you are dealing with a lot of fear in your life, I don't need to have been there, listening to all your thoughts, to know what you have been thinking on. You have been thinking upon things that weren't good, that weren't godly, that weren't holy, that weren't based on the Word of God, and now we can see the fruit.

- If you start thinking like a sick person, you're going to start behaving like a sick person.

- We have to change the way we think about healing. We have to change the way we approach the Word of God. It isn't just a Band-Aid® for when something goes wrong.

- We could go out into the streets today and lay hands on unbelievers and see miraculous healing. But if they want to permanently walk in health, they will have to come to know Jesus in an intimate way.

- Thoughts are like planes that are circling around. There may be negative thoughts, planes, in your airspace, but you don't have to give those thoughts permission to land in your heart.

- Peace is the antidote to depression, anxiety, worry, fear, and confusion. You received the Prince of Peace when you received Jesus. Peace is part of your new nature.

- You can't ask the Holy Spirit to bring out of your heart what you haven't first planted there.

- If you want to renew your mind to the Word of God, it means meditating on the scripture and speaking it out of your mouth, studying it, uttering it, and roaring it like a lion. That means speaking with authority.

- We need to lead our hearts by announcing over them, by proclaiming the Word over ourselves, our lives, our kids, our bodies, our finances, and our relationships. We need to start calling them blessed.

- Keep the Word of God that you've heard today. The word *keep* means to cling to. We are to hold fast to the Word, to seize it, to retain it in our hearts. Then when trouble comes, you possess the truth.

GO DEEPER

Self-Examination Questions

What negative words have you been speaking, and what are the roots of those words?

What wrong thinking has led to doubt and fear in your life? What right thinking will lead you to faith and a sound mind?

What areas of your thought life will you need to take captive? How will you do that?

On a scale from 1–10 (low to high), how willing are you to commit to monitoring your thoughts and what you are speaking?

Prayer Points

Use these prayer points to write and to pray your own powerful prayer:

- Thank God for loving you.
- Thank God for His Word that has all of the answers you need to have a sound mind.
- Ask God to reveal areas of your heart where you have kept Him out and where you have been wounded and haven't allowed Him in.
- Thank the Holy Spirit for being your comforter, your helper, and your friend.
- Ask God to reveal to you your thought patterns and belief systems that haven't been based upon the Word of God.
- Praise God for giving you tools to renew your mind.
- Declare that you will meditate on and speak out the Word of God.
- Confess times when you have allowed fear to guide your thoughts.
- Ask the Holy Spirit to guide you to truth in God's Word.

Action Steps

- In your Healing University journal, write the words that have come out of your mouth throughout the day. Look back and see whether the words were positive or negative. Begin to track the negative or critical words and try to discover their roots. In the margin, write some of the sources of these negative words. Also keep track of the bad fruit that is produced from those negative words, such as an argument or physical ailment. Use a highlighter to illuminate your positive words and note the good fruit from those words. Keep track daily of your words until you begin to see fewer or no negative words.

- In this lesson, Carlie suggested using index cards to write out Bible verses to use like a weapon against the negative thoughts of the enemy. She suggested that you pray in tongues and ask God to give you some scriptures. Let the Holy Spirit inspire you. You may want to paper hole punch the corner of each index card and put the cards on a large metal clasp or ring. Carry the cards with you to flip through and study whenever you have a few minutes.

- Settle in your heart that God wants you mentally prosperous. You cannot expect to walk in mental health and healing without first changing your thinking and your speaking to line up with what the Word of God says. Examine your heart and, when you are ready, make the following declaration and don't waver from it:

  I believe that my mental prosperity comes through renewing my mind and speaking God's Word. _____ (sign and date)

- Write your own answer to this question: *How can I improve my mental health?*

Additional Resource:

Carlie mentioned the Confession Card of promises from the Word of God. Please contact her ministry at **terradezministries.com** to obtain your copy.

Need prayer?

Please call **719-635-1111** for prayer or for more information on Charis Bible College.

awmi.net | charisbiblecollege.org

SCRIPTURES

Mental Health

Proverbs 23:7

For as he thinks in his heart, so is he. "Eat and drink!" he says to you, But his heart is not with you.

3 John 2

Beloved, I pray that you may prosper in all things and be in health, just as your soul prospers.

Matthew 12:34

Brood of vipers! How can you, being evil, speak good things? For out of the abundance of the heart the mouth speaks.

Luke 6:45

A good man out of the good treasure of his heart brings forth good; and an evil man out of the evil treasure of his heart brings forth evil. For out of the abundance of the heart his mouth speaks.

Romans 12:1–2

I beseech you therefore, brethren, by the mercies of God, that you present your bodies a living sacrifice, holy, acceptable to God, which is your reasonable service. And do not be conformed to this world, but be transformed by the renewing of your mind, that you may prove what is that good and acceptable and perfect will of God.

2 Timothy 1:7

For God has not given us a spirit of fear, but of power and of love and of a sound mind.

Mark 4:19

And the cares of this world, the deceitfulness of riches, and the desires for other things entering in choke the word, and it becomes unfruitful.

Mark 11:22–23

So Jesus answered and said to them, "I have faith in God. For assuredly, I say to you, whoever says to this mountain, 'Be removed and be cast into the sea,' and does not doubt in his heart, but believes that those things he says will be done, he will have whatever he says.

Galatians 5:1

Stand fast therefore in the liberty by which Christ has made us free, and do not be entangled again with a yoke of bondage.

2 Corinthians 10:3–6

For though we walk in the flesh, we do not war according to the flesh. For the weapons of our warfare are not carnal but mighty in God for pulling down strongholds, casting down arguments and every high thing that exalts itself against the knowledge of God, bringing every thought into captivity to the obedience of Christ, and being ready to punish all disobedience when your obedience is fulfilled.

Hebrews 4:15

For we do not have a High Priest who cannot sympathize with our weaknesses, but was in all points tempted as we are, yet without sin.

John 10:10

The thief does not come except to steal, and to kill, and to destroy. I have come that they may have life, and that they may have it more abundantly.

Hebrews 2:14–15

Inasmuch then as the children have partaken of flesh and blood, He Himself likewise shared in the same, that through death He might destroy him who had the power of death, that is, the devil, and release those who through fear of death were all their lifetime subject to bondage.

Isaiah 26:3

You will keep him in perfect peace, Whose mind is stayed on You, Because he trusts in You.

2 Corinthians 10:5

Casting down arguments and every high thing that exalts itself against the knowledge of God, bringing every thought into captivity to the obedience of Christ.

Galatians 5:22–23

But the fruit of the Spirit is love, joy, peace, longsuffering, kindness, goodness, faith-fulness, gentleness, self-control. Against such there is no law.

Philippians 4:6–9

Be anxious for nothing, but in everything by prayer and supplication, with thanksgiving, let your requests be made known to God; and the peace of God, which surpasses all understanding, will guard your hearts and minds through Christ Jesus. Finally, brethren, whatever things are true, whatever things are noble, whatever things are just, whatever things are pure, whatever things are lovely, whatever things are of good report, if there is any virtue and if there is anything praiseworthy—meditate on these things. The things which you learned and received and heard and saw in me, these do, and the God of peace will be with you.

Joshua 1:8–9

This Book of the Law shall not depart from your mouth, but you shall meditate in it day and night, that you may observe to do according to all that is written in it. For then you will make your way prosperous, and then you will have good success. Have I not commanded you? Be strong and of good courage; do not be afraid, nor be dismayed, for the LORD your God is with you wherever you go."

Proverbs 23:15–16

My son, if your heart is wise, My heart will rejoice—indeed, I myself; Yes, my inmost being will rejoice When your lips speak right things.

Proverbs 22:19

Hear, my son, and be wise; And guide your heart in the way.

2 Timothy 1:13–14

Hold fast the pattern of sound words which you have heard from me, in faith and love which are in Christ Jesus. That good thing which was committed to you, keep by the Holy Spirit who dwells in us.

Luke 8:18

Therefore take heed how you hear. For whoever has, to him more will be given; and whoever does not have, even what he seems to have will be taken from him."

Mark 4:24

Then He said to them, "Take heed what you hear. With the same measure you use, it will be measured to you; and to you who hear, more will be given."

Luke 8:12–15

Those by the wayside are the ones who hear; then the devil comes and takes away the word out of their hearts, lest they should believe and be saved. But the ones on the rock are those who, when they hear, receive the word with joy; and these have no root, who believe for a while and in time of temptation fall away. Now the ones that fell among thorns are those who, when they have heard, go out and are choked with cares, riches, and pleasures of life, and bring no fruit to maturity. But the ones that fell on the good ground are those who, having heard the word with a noble and good heart, keep it and bear fruit with patience.

Lesson 10
Emotional and Relational Health
Instructor
Daniel Amstutz

Note: All scriptures used in this lesson are quoted from the *New King James Version*.

I.   All of us have felt the effects of stress in our lives—stress really is a killer. *Perilous* means stressful, difficult, and hard to deal with.

> *But know this, that in the last days perilous times will come.*
>
> 2 Timothy 3:1

A. If we don't deal with stress according to the Word and Spirit of God, it can really start to add up in our hearts until we feel like we don't know where we're going and we have lost our way.

B. People often suffer in silence with an overloaded heart, a heart that is stressed out because they don't know what to do.

C. Have you ever made vows like, "No one is ever going to hurt me again," in an effort to self-protect? The problem with those kinds of vows is that they become access points for the enemy into your soul because you are self-protecting instead of letting the Lord be your protector.

D. Strongholds made from unresolved issues don't protect you—they isolate you. They literally become high towers of brokenness that end up isolating your heart.

E. Most church people would easily recognize carousing and drunkenness, but we sadly miss it many times in "the cares of this life." We've learned to live with toxic levels of stress. We've let the cares of this life enter in and choke the Word until it becomes unfruitful in the soil of our hearts.

> *And the cares of this world, the deceitfulness of riches, and the desires for other things entering in choke the word, and it becomes unfruitful.*
>
> Mark 4:19

II. God's compassion and love are the keys to living life with passion, and that's really what God wants for you. He wants you to live this life in the abundance of the grace of God.

A. We can offload our care because God cares for us.

Casting all your care upon Him, for He cares for you.

1 Peter 5:7

B. If you think you can carry your care, then you're trusting in yourself, not the Lord. Trusting in yourself is the root of self-centeredness.

C. Through unbelief, you'll eventually develop a hardened heart. These issues are easier to deal with when they're small, so don't let these things grow up in your temple like they belong there. If you do, eventually they become a stumbling block to your heart.

III. Your temple belongs to the Holy Ghost, and God wants your temple to be filled with Him, not all this other stuff. Living with an overloaded heart will never be the will of God. God wants you living with passion.

I know your works, that you are neither cold nor hot. I could wish you were cold or hot. So then, because you are lukewarm, and neither cold nor hot, I will vomit you out of My mouth.

Revelation 3:15–16

A. God gives grace to the humble, the teachable, and God's grace has everything that we need.

But He gives more grace. Therefore He says: "God resists the proud, But gives grace to the humble."

James 4:6

IV. Mental and emotional healing are included in the Atonement and are very important to the heart of God.

He heals the brokenhearted And binds up their wounds.

Psalms 147:3

A. Healing for the brokenhearted was so important to the heart of God that it is the first mention of healing in the New Covenant.

"The Spirit of the LORD is upon Me, Because He has anointed Me To preach the gospel to the poor; He has sent Me to heal the brokenhearted, To proclaim liberty to the captives And recovery of sight to the blind, To set at liberty those who are oppressed; To proclaim the acceptable year of the LORD." Then He closed the book, and gave it back to the attendant and sat down. And the eyes of all who were in the synagogue were fixed on Him. And He began to say to them, "Today this Scripture is fulfilled in your hearing."

Luke 4:18–21

B. We are literally the gardeners of our hearts.

Keep your heart with all diligence, For out of it spring the issues of life.

Proverbs 4:23

C. Disappointments can easily turn into disillusionment, which leads to a disconnect.

Hope deferred makes the heart sick, But when the desire comes, it is a tree of life.

Proverbs 13:12

D. We get into these situations at times where we feel like we have to carry our grief and emotional trauma, and we don't know what to do.

Surely He has borne our griefs And carried our sorrows; Yet we esteemed Him stricken, Smitten by God, and afflicted. But He was wounded for our transgressions, He was bruised for our iniquities; The chastisement for our peace was upon Him, And by His stripes we are healed.

Isaiah 53:4–5

E. Don't harden your heart to God; realize that God is your answer.

The LORD is near to those who have a broken heart, And saves such as have a contrite spirit.

Psalms 34:18

F. God doesn't want what's lame to be dislocated; He wants it to be healed.

Therefore strengthen the hands which hang down, and the feeble knees, and make straight paths for your feet, so that what is lame may not be dislocated, but rather be healed.

Hebrews 12:12–13

G. A root of bitterness is an unresolved heart issue. Left unresolved, it will spring up and defile many.

Pursue peace with all people, *and holiness, without which no one will see the Lord: looking carefully lest anyone fall short of the grace of God; lest any root of bitterness springing up cause trouble, and by this many become defiled.*

Hebrews 12:14–15

V. The Word of God will actually separate spirit, soul, and body and show us what we need to see to be able to offload—get rid of—anything negative and replace it with the Word of God.

For the word of God is living and powerful, and sharper than any two-edged sword, piercing even to the division of soul and spirit, and of joints and marrow, and is a discerner of the thoughts and intents of the heart.

Hebrews 4:12

A. Emotional and mental healing take place in the area of our being called the soul, which is where we locate our mind, our will, and our emotions. Our emotions will follow our thoughts, and our thoughts are the result of what we decide to think on. In order to change your life, you're going to have to change how you're thinking.

Finally, brethren, whatever things are true, whatever things are *noble, whatever things* are *just, whatever things* are *pure, whatever things* are *lovely, whatever things* are *of good report, if* there is *any virtue and if* there is *anything praiseworthy— meditate on these things.*

Philippians 4:8

B. God's will is for all of us to prosper and be in health in every area of our lives. So, emotional well-being is more important than most people realize. Many in our generation are stressed out much of the time and think their stressed-out lifestyle is normal or natural.

Beloved, I pray that you may prosper in all things and be in health, just as your soul prospers.

3 John 2

VI. Psychology attempts to heal, but it can only deal with the natural, only with the soul and the body. Only through Jesus do we find supernatural healing of all three parts: the spirit, the soul, and the body. He, as the healer, makes sure that it works.

For God has not given us a spirit of fear, but of power and of love and of a sound mind.

2 Timothy 1:7

A. We see through our beliefs into our daily lives. There's something about life that's just so daily! What you do every day matters more than what you do every now and then. Allow the Holy Spirit to help you see right now from God's perspective, which will always start from the inside out. It will always involve the heart.

B. Past failure does not define who you are.

Brethren, I do not count myself to have apprehended; but one thing I do, forgetting those things which are behind and reaching forward to those things which are ahead.

Philippians 3:13

C. You can be healed of trauma, emotional pain, and mental disorder to the point that you no longer even identify with it anymore.

VII. The victory of Jesus is literally the place we start because His victory was for us. It's what the New Covenant is all about. He overcame, so now we can overcome.

And they overcame him by the blood of the Lamb and by the word of their testimony, and they did not love their lives to the death.

Revelations 12:11

A. We should be living life from our redeemed spirits, not from souls that want to be in control.

B. Everything God gave us when He created us, including our emotions, is good. God didn't make any junk, so don't let the enemy lie to you and tell you that you're damaged goods.

I will praise You, for I am fearfully and wonderfully made; Marvelous are Your works, And that my soul knows very well.

Psalms 139:14

C. There is no sickness or disease that is too hard for God, including emotional, mental, and relational healing.

VIII. Here are some practical things to help you receive emotional and mental healing:

A. Start on a daily basis by expressing gratitude, and be thankful because thanksgiving is the voice of faith.

Therefore by Him let us continually offer the sacrifice of praise to God, that is, the fruit of our lips, giving thanks to His name.

Hebrews 13:15

B. Renew your mind to the Word of God so that you can be transformed and not conformed.

I beseech you therefore, brethren, by the mercies of God, that you present your bodies a living sacrifice, holy, acceptable to God, which is your reasonable service. And do not be conformed to this world, but be transformed by the renewing of your mind, that you may prove what is that good and acceptable and perfect will of God.

Romans 12:1-2

C. Choose the one thing instead of one more thing.

And Jesus answered and said to her, "Martha, Martha, you are worried and troubled about many things. But one thing is needed, and Mary has chosen that good part, which will not be taken away from her."

Luke 10:41-42

D. Become quick to offload your heart through worship and prayer. Humble yourself and receive the grace that God has for you.

E. Build yourself up on your most holy faith by praying in tongues, and do it a lot!

> *But you, beloved, building yourselves up on your most holy faith, praying in the Holy Spirit.*
>
> Jude 20

F. If you have unforgiveness toward someone who hurt you, lay it down by trusting Jesus with whatever wounded you. Letting it go doesn't mean that they were right.

IX. For relational healing, we need to walk in an attitude of forgiveness, rather than taking hurt into our hearts as if we're going to own it for the rest of our lives.

A. Ephesians 5 is talking about relationships and the importance of healing relationships. It is important to submit in the grace of God in a way that never puts people down, but actually does the opposite: lifts them up into their potential and destiny.

B. Many times, married men don't realize how important it is to dwell with their wives with understanding. Figure out what makes her tick, what her loves are, and what you can do to be a blessing to her.

> *Husbands, likewise, dwell with* them *with understanding, giving honor to the wife, as to the weaker vessel, and as* being *heirs together of the grace of life, that your prayers may not be hindered.*
>
> 1 Peter 3:7

C. You can help relational healing flow when you are heirs together of the grace of life.

> *Finally, all of you be of one mind, having compassion for one another; love as broth-ers,* be *tenderhearted,* be *courteous; not returning evil for evil or reviling for reviling, but on the contrary blessing, knowing that you were called to this, that you may inherit a blessing.*
>
> 1 Peter 3:8–9

D. Sin and guilt love to work in secret. When we confess our sins to another person, somebody who's trustworthy, we make ourselves vulnerable. We have to humble ourselves to that brother or sister in the Lord and receive healing from the Lord Jesus through them.

Is anyone among you suffering? Let him pray. Is anyone cheerful? Let him sing psalms. Is anyone among you sick? Let him call for the elders of the church, and let them pray over him, anointing him with oil in the name of the Lord. And the prayer of faith will save the sick, and the Lord will raise him up. And if he has committed sins, he will be forgiven. Confess your trespasses to one another, and pray for one another, that you may be healed. The effective fervent prayer of a righteous man avails much.

James 5:13–16

LESSON REVIEW QUESTIONS

1. What might result from an unwillingness to deal with stress?

2. How should a Christian deal with stress?

3. Describe what a believer's heart should be full of and what it should not have in it.

4. Where does the Bible address emotional healing?

5. What relational healing advice is given in Hebrews 12:14–15?

6. What are six practical ways to receive emotional and mental healing?

**LESSON REVIEW
ANSWERS**

1.   What might result from an unwillingness to deal with stress?

     Possible answers: A person might feel lost; the stress can weigh down our hearts and cause a person to not know what to do; the cares of the world can choke the Word until it becomes unfruitful in our hearts.

2.   How should a Christian deal with stress?

     1 Peter 5:7 says we should cast our cares on Him because He cares for us.

3.   Describe what a believer's heart should be full of and what it should not have in it.

     A believer's heart should be full of the Holy Spirit and the fruit of the Spirit. A believer's heart should not be overloaded with cares of the world or be hardened, because a hardened heart opens the door to the enemy.

4.   Where does the Bible address emotional healing?

     Possible answers: Psalms 147:3 says He heals the brokenhearted; in Luke 4:18–21 Jesus says He heals the brokenhearted; Proverbs 13:12 shows how hope deferred makes the heart sick; Psalms 34:18 says He is near those who have a broken heart.

5.   What relational healing advice is given in Hebrews 12:14–15?

     Hebrews 12:14–15 says to pursue peace and not to let bitterness take root in our hearts or we will defile others also.

6.   What are six practical ways to receive emotional and mental healing?

     1. **Start on a daily basis by expressing gratitude and being thankful, because thanksgiving is the voice of faith.**

     2. **Renew your mind to the Word of God so that you can be transformed and not conformed.**

     3. **Choose the one thing instead of one more thing.**

4. Become quick to offload your heart through worship and prayer. Humble yourself and receive the grace that God has for you.

5. Build yourself up on your most holy faith by praying in tongues, and do it a lot.

6. If you have unforgiveness toward someone who hurt you, lay it down by trusting Jesus with whatever wounded you. Letting it go doesn't mean that they were right.

Need prayer?

Please call **719-635-1111** for prayer or for more information on Charis Bible College.

awmi.net | charisbiblecollege.org

POINTS TO PONDER

- Unresolved issues of the heart are the result of an unrenewed mind repeatedly processing toxic thoughts, which turn into reasonings and eventually become strongholds.

- When you get a revelation of how much God loves you, it's like you suddenly get 20/20 vision. It's like everything becomes clear.

- Going numb and shutting down emotionally is not spiritual; it's actually emotional illness. Shifting your heart into neutral is what makes you lukewarm, and living life in neutral is not what you want to do.

- God wants you to be well more than you do.

- When our talk and our walk are different, when they don't agree, it begins to affect others who are around us.

- If you want to know what's really in your heart, listen to your mouth.

- God not only wants you to have a renewed mind, but He also wants your soul to be restored. God wants you to be living beside still waters with the life peace of God flowing up from within you, blessing your life in every single way—prospering and being in health.

- Prospering and being in health includes the whole man: spirit, soul, and body.

- You're supposed to be living from the fruit of the Spirit on the inside of you, not living with an overloaded heart.

- Live your life in such a way that you don't live with a troubled heart, but learn to offload your heart at the throne of grace.

- Instead of wanting good but expecting bad, your heart can be so transformed that you begin to relate to daily life in a completely different way.

- Not knowing how to live life in Christ, with the fruit of the Spirit alive on the inside of you, can be very crippling and destructive.

- God doesn't want the New Covenant in your spirit and the Old Covenant in your body.

- When you start to get filled with the Holy Ghost, it pushes all that other stuff out of your soul.

- Holding on to bitterness or unforgiveness is often a doorway to the enemy, so shut that door by letting it go, once and for all.

- If you don't want your prayer life to be hindered as a husband, then you better take heed. As a husband, you should be kind and gentle and honor your wife as your best friend. Listen to her, spend time with her, love her, and cherish her.

- When you confess your sins to someone, the Lord in them is ministering through them to you. They are not the healer, but Jesus in them is—so a relational healing can happen.

GO DEEPER

Self-Examination Questions

Do you really believe your emotional and relational issues affect your health? If so, how?

What stresses do you allow in your life? Do you consider them normal? Will you continue to allow them? Why or why not?

On a scale from 1–10 (low to high), how willing are you to commit to unloading your stress and emotional burdens on Jesus? What is your plan for unloading them?

Prayer Points

Use these prayer points to write and to pray your own powerful prayer:

- Praise God that He gave you a sound mind.
- Ask God to reveal to you stresses and unresolved issues that you have allowed to burden your heart.
- Thank Jesus for the Atonement that bought emotional and relational healing for you.
- Repent of tolerating situations instead of releasing them to God.
- Thank God that He restores your soul.
- Thank God that He does not want you to live with a troubled heart.
- Thank God that repentance binds Satan.
- Declare that fear and torment are cast out because of God's perfect love.
- Release bitterness and unforgiveness.
- Command emotional and relational healing.
- Praise God that when you humbly confess your sins to another, the Lord ministers healing to you through them.

Action Steps

- In your Healing University journal, create a visual representation of the stress you hold on to. Divide the page in half. Draw a small heart at the bottom of the left side of the page. Prayerfully ask God to reveal to you what you are holding on to and allowing to weigh down your heart. Write each issue, person, situation, offense, fear, and item

God reveals on a line above the heart going up the page. Do you see how these weigh down your heart? Now on the right hand side, draw a heart at the very top of the page. Beside each item listed on the left side, write what God's Word says about it, or the truth about what God says about you. Do you see how your heart can soar when you release each item to God and let His peace reign?

- Settle in your heart that God desires for you to have emotional and relational healing through releasing the stresses and cares of this life to Him. Examine your heart and, when you are ready, make the following declaration and don't waver from it:

I believe God desires for me to have emotional and relational healing now as I release the stresses and cares of this life to Him.

_____ (sign and date)

- Write your own answer to this question: *What needs to change so I will experience emotional and relational healing?*

SCRIPTURES

Emotional and Relational Health

2 Timothy 3:1

> *But know this, that in the last days perilous times will come.*

Isaiah 61:3

> *To console those who mourn in Zion, To give them beauty for ashes, The oil of joy for mourning, The garment of praise for the spirit of heaviness; That they may be called trees of righteousness, The planting of the LORD, that He may be glorified.*

Luke 21:33–38

> *"Heaven and earth will pass away, but My words will by no means pass away. But take heed to yourselves, lest your hearts be weighed down with carousing, drunkenness, and cares of this life, and that Day come on you unexpectedly. For it will come as a snare on all those who dwell on the face of the whole earth. Watch therefore, and pray always that you may be counted worthy to escape all these things that will come to pass, and to stand before the Son of Man." And in the daytime He was teaching in the temple, but at night He went out and stayed on the mountain called Olivet. Then early in the morning all the people came to Him in the temple to hear Him.*

Mark 4:19

> *And the cares of this world, the deceitfulness of riches, and the desires for other things entering in choke the word, and it becomes unfruitful.*

1 Peter 5:7

> *Casting all your care upon Him, for He cares for you.*

Revelation 3:15–16

> *I know your works, that you are neither cold nor hot. I could wish you were cold or hot. So then, because you are lukewarm, and neither cold nor hot, I will vomit you out of My mouth.*

1 Peter 5:5

Likewise you younger people, submit yourselves to your elders. Yes, all of you be submissive to one another, and be clothed with humility, for "God resists the proud, But gives grace to the humble."

James 4:6

But He gives more grace. Therefore He says: "God resists the proud, But gives grace to the humble."

John 10:10

The thief does not come except to steal, and to kill, and to destroy. I have come that they may have life, and that they may have it more abundantly.

1 John 4:17

Love has been perfected among us in this: that we may have boldness in the day of judgment; because as He is, so are we in this world.

Psalms 147:3

He heals the brokenhearted And binds up their wounds.

Luke 4:18–21

"The Spirit of the LORD is upon Me, Because He has anointed Me To preach the gospel to the poor; He has sent Me to heal the brokenhearted, To proclaim liberty to the captives And recovery of sight to the blind, To set at liberty those who are oppressed; To proclaim the acceptable year of the LORD." Then He closed the book, and gave it back to the attendant and sat down. And the eyes of all who were in the synagogue were fixed on Him. And He began to say to them, "Today this Scripture is fulfilled in your hearing."

Proverbs 4:23

Keep your heart with all diligence, For out of it spring the issues of life.

Proverbs 13:12

Hope deferred makes the heart sick, But when the desire comes, it is a tree of life.

Isaiah 53:4-5

Surely He has borne our griefs And carried our sorrows; Yet we esteemed Him stricken, Smitten by God, and afflicted. But He was *wounded for our transgressions, He was bruised for our iniquities; The chastisement for our peace* was *upon Him, And by His stripes we are healed.*

Psalms 34:18

The Lord *is near to those who have a broken heart, And saves such as have a contrite spirit.*

Hebrews 12:12-13

Therefore strengthen the hands which hang down, and the feeble knees, and make straight paths for your feet, so that what is lame may not be dislocated, but rather be healed.

Hebrews 12:14-15

Pursue peace with all people, *and holiness, without which no one will see the Lord: looking carefully lest anyone fall short of the grace of God; lest any root of bitterness springing up cause trouble, and by this many become defiled.*

John 4:14

But whoever drinks of the water that I shall give him will never thirst. But the water that I shall give him will become in him a fountain of water springing up into everlasting life.

John 7:38

He who believes in Me, as the Scripture has said, out of his heart will flow rivers of living water.

Matthew 12:34

Brood of vipers! How can you, being evil, speak good things? For out of the abundance of the heart the mouth speaks.

1 Peter 3:4

Rather let it be the hidden person of the heart, with the incorruptible beauty of a gentle and quiet spirit, which is very precious in the sight of God.

1 Thessalonians 5:23

Now may the God of peace Himself sanctify you completely; and may your whole spirit, soul, and body be preserved blameless at the coming of our Lord Jesus Christ.

Hebrews 4:12

For the word of God is living and powerful, and sharper than any two-edged sword, piercing even to the division of soul and spirit, and of joints and marrow, and is a discerner of the thoughts and intents of the heart.

Psalms 103:1–3

Bless the LORD, O my soul; And all that is within me, bless His holy name! Bless the LORD, O my soul, And forget not all His benefits: Who forgives all your iniquities, Who heals all your diseases.

2 Corinthians 5:17

Therefore, if anyone is in Christ, he is a new creation; old things have passed away; behold, all things have become new.

Philippians 4:8

Finally, brethren, whatever things are true, whatever things are noble, whatever things are just, whatever things are pure, whatever things are lovely, whatever things are of good report, if there is any virtue and if there is anything praiseworthy— meditate on these things.

3 John 2

Beloved, I pray that you may prosper in all things and be in health, just as your soul prospers.

Proverbs 17:22

A merry heart does good, like medicine, But a broken spirit dries the bones.

Philippians 4:6

Be anxious for nothing, but in everything by prayer and supplication, with thanksgiving, let your requests be made known to God.

2 Timothy 1:7

For God has not given us a spirit of fear, but of power and of love and of a sound mind.

James 4:2

> *You lust and do not have. You murder and covet and cannot obtain. You fight and war. Yet you do not have because you do not ask.*

John 14:13–14

> *And whatever you ask in My name, that I will do, that the Father may be glorified in the Son. If you ask anything in My name, I will do it.*

Philippians 4:7

> *And the peace of God, which surpasses all understanding, will guard your hearts and minds through Christ Jesus.*

John 14:1

> *Let not your heart be troubled; you believe in God, believe also in Me.*

Proverbs 23:7

> *For as he thinks in his heart, so is he. "Eat and drink!" he says to you, But his heart is not with you.*

Matthew 6:11

> *Give us this day our daily bread.*

Psalms 118: 24

> *This is the day the LORD has made; We will rejoice and be glad in it.*

Philippians 3:13

> *Brethren, I do not count myself to have apprehended; but one thing I do, forgetting those things which are behind and reaching forward to those things which are ahead.*

John 16:33

> *These things I have spoken to you, that in Me you may have peace. In the world you will have tribulation; but be of good cheer, I have overcome the world.*

Revelations 12:11

> *And they overcame him by the blood of the Lamb and by the word of their testimony, and they did not love their lives to the death.*

Genesis 1:31

> *Then God saw everything that He had made, and indeed it was very good. So the evening and the morning were the sixth day.*

Psalms 139:14

> *I will praise You, for I am fearfully and wonderfully made; Marvelous are Your works, And that my soul knows very well.*

Mark 16:18

> *They will take up serpents; and if they drink anything deadly, it will by no means hurt them; they will lay hands on the sick, and they will recover.*

John 19:30

> *So when Jesus had received the sour wine, He said, "It is finished!" And bowing His head, He gave up His spirit.*

Philippians 2:9

> *Therefore God also has highly exalted Him and given Him the name which is above every name.*

Hebrews 13:15

> *Therefore by Him let us continually offer the sacrifice of praise to God, that is, the fruit of our lips, giving thanks to His name.*

Romans 12:1–2

> *I beseech you therefore, brethren, by the mercies of God, that you present your bodies a living sacrifice, holy, acceptable to God, which is your reasonable service. And do not be conformed to this world, but be transformed by the renewing of your mind, that you may prove what is that good and acceptable and perfect will of God.*

Luke 10:41–42

> *And Jesus answered and said to her, "Martha, Martha, you are worried and troubled about many things. But one thing is needed, and Mary has chosen that good part, which will not be taken away from her."*

Jude 20

But you, beloved, building yourselves up on your most holy faith, praying in the Holy Spirit.

Luke 17:1–5

Then He said to the disciples, "It is impossible that no offenses should come, but woe to him through whom they do come! It would be better for him if a millstone were hung around his neck, and he were thrown into the sea, than that he should offend one of these little ones. Take heed to yourselves. If your brother sins against you, rebuke him; and if he repents, forgive him. And if he sins against you seven times in a day, and seven times in a day returns to you, saying, 'I repent,' you shall forgive him." And the apostles said to the Lord, "Increase our faith."

Matthew 18:22

Jesus said to him, "I do not say to you, up to seven times, but up to seventy times seven."

Ephesians 5:22–23

Wives, submit to your own husbands, as to the Lord. For the husband is head of the wife, as also Christ is head of the church; and He is the Savior of the body.

1 Peter 3:7

Husbands, likewise, dwell with them *with understanding, giving honor to the wife, as to the weaker vessel, and as* being *heirs together of the grace of life, that your prayers may not be hindered.*

1 Peter 3:8–9

Finally, all of you be *of one mind, having compassion for one another; love as brothers, be tenderhearted, be courteous; not returning evil for evil or reviling for reviling, but on the contrary blessing, knowing that you were called to this, that you may inherit a blessing.*

James 5:13–16

Is anyone among you suffering? Let him pray. Is anyone cheerful? Let him sing psalms. Is anyone among you sick? Let him call for the elders of the church, and let them pray over him, anointing him with oil in the name of the Lord. And the prayer of faith will save the sick, and the Lord will raise him up. And if he has committed sins, he will be forgiven. Confess your trespasses to one another, and pray for one another, that you may be healed. The effective fervent prayer of a righteous man avails much.

Lesson 11
Is My Diet Important?
Instructor:
Carrie Pickett

Note: All scriptures used in this lesson are quoted from the *New King James Version*.

I.   The whole spirit, soul, and body dynamic indicates God creates things after His own image. He is made of God the Father, God the Son, and God the Holy Spirit. So, God created you as a three-part being that He could demonstrate and live through all aspects.

> *Now may the God of peace Himself sanctify you completely; and may your whole spirit, soul, and body be preserved blameless at the coming of our Lord Jesus Christ.*
> 1 Thessalonians 5:23

   A. Your body is a temple of the Holy Spirit. That means we've got to steward it and give it to the leadership of Jesus Christ.

> *I have been crucified with Christ; it is no longer I who live, but Christ lives in me; and the* life *which I now live in the flesh I live by faith in the Son of God, who loved me and gave Himself for me.*
> Galatians 2:20

II. Many people say, "I want Jesus, but I want to live like I want to in this world."

   A. We overcome because of what Jesus did—by the blood of the Lamb. Because of the word of the testimony and what He's actively producing within my life, I have given my life so radically to the ownership of Jesus that I'm willing to die for Christ.

> *And they overcame him by the blood of the Lamb and by the word of their testimony, and they did not love their lives to the death.*
> Revelation 12:11

B. There's the dynamic that I have power, life, and victory in this finished work of God inside of me, but there's also the wisdom of stewardship over what God has entrusted me with in this body.

III. There are extreme dynamics that people will go to.

A. You can start to operate in a level of fear that every time you eat something, you're going to get cancer. Watch your words. There's life and death in the power of your words. Do not speak death over your body, and do not speak death over your children's bodies.

Death and life are in the power of the tongue, And those who love it will eat its fruit.
                                                                        Proverbs 18:21

B. When Jesus walked the earth, there was no processed food, yet He still went about healing the sick.

C. Understand sickness. The enemy doesn't care what your diet is; no matter how well you take care of your body, he wants to kill, steal, and destroy.

The thief does not come except to steal, and to kill, and to destroy. I have come that they may have life, and that they may have it more abundantly.
                                                                        John 10:10

D. You can believe all sickness comes from food, so you worry and are aggressive regarding food because of fear. Or you can do a pendulum swing and go the other way: you can believe all sickness comes from the devil, so you just rebuke him and eat whatever you want, thinking it doesn't matter.

E. Find a balance between the two. Yes, God only looks at the spirit, but recognize there might be some unhealthy things out there. Ask the Lord for wisdom.

IV. Don't just think that your diet is the only thing that matters.

But He answered and said, "It is written, 'Man shall not live by bread alone, but by every word that proceeds from the mouth of God.'"
                                                                        Matthew 4:4

A. It's not just the bread you eat, it's the understanding the Word of God that sustains you and gives you wisdom for how to walk in this present life.

B. Because of the lies of the enemy, you and I can make some bad choices with our health and accept sickness.

V. Just like God's grace and forgiveness are enough to forgive us of our sins, God's grace and power are able to heal our bodies from bad choices.

A. Say, "Lord, despite my bad choices, You can heal my body." The same grace that redeems your spirit and transforms your mind has the ability to equip you in your body now as a temple of the Holy Spirit.

For the grace of God that brings salvation has appeared to all men, teaching us that, denying ungodliness and worldly lusts, we should live soberly, righteously, and godly in the present age, looking for the blessed hope and glorious appearing of our great God and Savior Jesus Christ, who gave Himself for us, that He might redeem us from every lawless deed and purify for Himself His own special people, zealous for good works.

Titus 2:11–14

B. Wake up in the morning and say, "Lord, what's Your plan? How do You want me to live today? What do You want me to do?"

C. If you aren't healthy, you'll come to places of wisdom and opportunity, but your physical body won't be able to let you walk into them.

D. Some people will allow age to disqualify them from certain opportunities or believe, "When I get older, I won't be able to do those things." We, with the grace of God, can learn to steward our temple.

E. There are things that God has planned for you, and you have disqualified yourself because you've accepted that your body would never allow you to do it. You can experience a miracle. The grace of God and the leading and guiding of the Holy Spirit can teach you how to lead your body, how to eat, how to sleep, how to rest, and how to steward your temple so that you're ready for God's plans.

F. There is wisdom that God can give you right now. You don't have to be frustrated that you're too far gone. Start today.

VI. Ask the Holy Spirit, "Could You help me make wise decisions today?"

> *When He had called the multitude to Himself, He said to them, "Hear and under-stand: Not what goes into the mouth defiles a man; but what comes out of the mouth, this defiles a man."*
>
> Matthew 15:10–11

A. God can teach you what to eat. God wants to teach your heart. More than just surrendering your diet to the Lord, are you willing to surrender your life to Him?

B. In the same way we talk about finances, relationships, callings, jobs, and purpose, let's bring our diets and bodies into surrender to God and say, "Lord, if there's something that needs to be adjusted in my life, here it is. I give it to You."

C. Rest is important to God because if you are not rested, it is much easier to get into the flesh.

D. Be wise with your time.

> *See then that you walk circumspectly, not as fools but as wise, redeeming the time, because the days are evil.*
>
> Ephesians 5:15–16

E. There's a rhythm for your diet, your body, and your exercise that God has for you—find this balance.

F. All things are permissible, but not all things are beneficial. This means that if do not take care of your body, you're not going to feel well. You won't be able to walk through some of the doors that God has for you because the devil's going to tell you that your body's disqualifying you from the call of God on your life.

> *All things are lawful for me, but not all things are helpful; all things are lawful for me, but not all things edify.*
>
> 1 Corinthians 10:23

G. Your past doesn't define your future. Right now, make a decision and God can do some great things through you—spirit, soul and body—in this world, for such a time as this.

LESSON REVIEW QUESTIONS

1. Should Christians have a fear of what they eat? Why or why not?

2. Should Christians live without caring about diet or exercise? Why or why not?

3. What advice does Proverbs 18:21 give for dealing with your diet?

4. What are the two extreme views about diet?

5. What benefits can come from following God's wisdom about food and exercise?

6. How does 1 Corinthians 10:23 relate to diet and exercise?

7. What are some examples of diet or exercise problems that might limit a Christian's ability to accept ministry opportunities?

1.   Should Christians have a fear of what they eat? Why or why not?

   Possible answer: No; sicknesses are caused by the enemy, and we aren't to live in fear of what we eat because God's grace is greater than the enemy's lies that we deserve sickness because of what we eat.

2.   How should Christians view diet or exercise?

   Possible answer: Our bodies are temples of the Holy Spirit, and we should steward them well.

3.   What advice does Proverbs 18:21 give for dealing with your diet?

   Proverbs 18:21 warns to watch what you say about yourself and the food you eat. Don't speak or prophesy that foods will give you cancer or sickness.

4.   What are the two extreme views about diet?

   One extreme is to think that all sickness comes from my food, so I must be radical and fear food. Another extreme is to believe that all sickness is from the devil, who came to steal, kill, and destroy, so it doesn't matter what I eat.

5.   What benefits can come from following God's wisdom about food and exercise?

   Following God's wisdom about food and exercise will allow me to be fit and ready to walk through the doors of opportunity that God has planned for me.

6.   How does 1 Corinthians 10:23 relate to diet and exercise?

   Since 1 Corinthians 10:23 shows that all things are permissible but not beneficial, I can eat all foods, but they don't all benefit my health.

7.   What are some examples of diet or exercise problems that might limit a Christian's ability to accept ministry opportunities?

   Answers will vary.

POINTS TO PONDER

- Sometimes you can pray, preach, lay hands on people, evangelize, and look at your gifts, callings, passion, and love for God and not think that your physical life is important.

- We say, "I want Jesus in my heart, and I want to do what I want to do, when I want to do it, how I want to do it, and with whoever I want to do it with." Then we tag on, "Oh, by the way, God, could You please bless it, put Your stamp of approval on it, and send me money when I need it?"

- Let's not be so quick to attach every sickness to our food, to our water, and to chemicals. We need to recognize where sickness comes from—sickness comes from the devil.

- Understand that sickness is from the enemy, and rebuke it. Apply God's principles to your life. But at the same time, steward your temple, realizing that the life you now live, you live by the faith of the Son of God. You want your temple to be healthy and full of energy for the things that God has for you.

- If we are given a diagnosis, we listen to the lies of the enemy and automatically shake our heads and say, "Yeah, that makes sense because I've been not eating right. I deserve it. I did this to myself, so it makes sense that I need to live with it now."

- God is so good that He can redeem you from bad choices. We think that somehow we deserve sickness, so we receive the attack of the enemy to steal, kill, and destroy. We don't think that God could heal us because we did it to ourselves.

- You can be set free from the lie that says you deserve sickness and it will always be your burden to bear. Now you can start declaring, "No, I'm healed, and with that healing power comes the wisdom to make the right decisions."

- Even though you've made some bad decisions, if you're willing to hear God, He wants to teach you how to steward your temple.

- You can learn to steward your body in a way, led by relationship and intimacy with God, that your age, your strength, and your health will allow you to walk through the doors of opportunity that He planned for you before you were formed in your mother's womb.

- Say, "Lord, my life belongs to You, and therefore, the instruction that You bring me is for a reason. I'm going to let You deal with my heart."

- The Holy Spirit may show you things about your body that you need to do, and it might not make sense. If your life doesn't belong to you, and if God tells you to do something, obey it. You don't have to know all the reasons why.

- One of the most spiritual things you can do is take a nap! Sometimes we try to do everything in a day or don't steward our time wisely.

- You have the ability to hear God's voice, know it, and be guided by it to make daily decisions and changes. If you've been making mistakes and you have a lot of things you need to erase that have done things to your body, the grace of God, the power of God, and the healing work of Jesus can touch your body and teach you how to move forward.

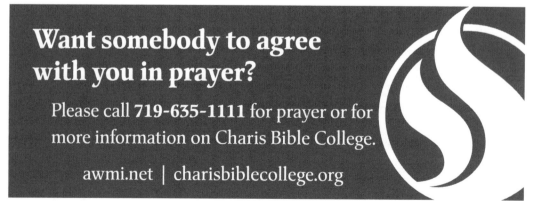

GO DEEPER

Self-Examination Questions

Do you really need to be concerned about your diet? Why or why not?

What lies about your diet have you believed? What truths and wisdom from God about your diet will replace those lies?

How will you take care of your body so that you can do what God has planned for you?

On a scale from 1–10 (low to high), how willing are you to commit to changing your diet to better steward your body as a temple of the Holy Spirit?

Prayer Points

Use these prayer points to write and to pray your own powerful prayer:

- Praise God that your body is the temple of the Holy Spirit.
- Repent of fear about food.
- Rebuke the lies from the enemy that say you deserve to be sick.
- Ask God to reveal to you wisdom in how to take care of your body.
- Commit to following the wisdom God gives you.
- Thank God that His grace for you includes healing your body.
- Thank Jesus for the opportunities He has planned for you.

Action Steps

- In your Healing University journal, write three ministry opportunities or ways you would like to serve God this week. Now make a list of foods you eat that build your body up to have strength and stamina to fulfill those opportunities. List foods you eat that do not build your body up and make you feel tired and run down. Ask God to bring you wisdom and resources to help you choose foods that will benefit your body. Write down each instruction and make a commitment to obey today!

- Do the same thing with your exercise and activities. What activities build strength and stamina to do the ministry God has called you to do?

- Settle in your heart that you are redeemed from the curse of sickness and God has grace for any past poor choices you have made. Your body is a temple, and God will give wisdom to you about caring for your body. Examine your heart and, when you are ready, make the following declaration and don't waver from it:

I believe my body is God's temple, and God has grace and wisdom for me to take care of my temple. _____ (sign and date)

- Write your own answer to this question: *Is my diet important?*

SCRIPTURES

Is My Diet Important?

Colossians 1:13

> *He has delivered us from the power of darkness and conveyed us into the kingdom of the Son of His love.*

1 Thessalonians 5:23

> *Now may the God of peace Himself sanctify you completely; and may your whole spirit, soul, and body be preserved blameless at the coming of our Lord Jesus Christ.*

Galatians 2:20

> *I have been crucified with Christ; it is no longer I who live, but Christ lives in me; and the life which I now live in the flesh I live by faith in the Son of God, who loved me and gave Himself for me.*

Matthew 16:24

> *Then Jesus said to His disciples, "If anyone desires to come after Me, let him deny himself, and take up his cross, and follow Me."*

Revelation 12:11

> *And they overcame him by the blood of the Lamb and by the word of their testimony, and they did not love their lives to the death.*

Proverbs 18:21

> *Death and life are in the power of the tongue, And those who love it will eat its fruit.*

John 10:10

> *The thief does not come except to steal, and to kill, and to destroy. I have come that they may have life, and that they may have it more abundantly.*

Matthew 4:4

> *But He answered and said, "It is written, 'Man shall not live by bread alone, but by every word that proceeds from the mouth of God.'"*

Titus 2:11–14

> *For the grace of God that brings salvation has appeared to all men, teaching us that, denying ungodliness and worldly lusts, we should live soberly, righteously, and godly in the present age, looking for the blessed hope and glorious appearing of our great God and Savior Jesus Christ, who gave Himself for us, that He might redeem us from every lawless deed and purify for Himself His own special people, zealous for good works.*

Matthew 15:10–11

> *When He had called the multitude to Himself, He said to them, "Hear and understand: Not what goes into the mouth defiles a man; but what comes out of the mouth, this defiles a man."*

Ephesians 5:15–16

> *See then that you walk circumspectly, not as fools but as wise, redeeming the time, because the days are evil.*

1 Corinthians 10:23

> *All things are lawful for me, but not all things are helpful; all things are lawful for me, but not all things edify.*

Lesson 12
How God Heals Part 1
Instructor
Greg Mohr

Note: All scriptures used in this lesson are quoted from the *New King James Version*.

I. Healing is the will of God for everyone, every time, all the time.

> *And it happened when He was in a certain city, that behold, a man who was full of leprosy saw Jesus; and he fell on his face and implored Him, saying, "Lord, if You are willing, You can make me clean." Then He put out His hand and touched him, saying, "I am willing; be cleansed." Immediately the leprosy left him.*
>
> Luke 5:12–13

A. It really takes no faith to believe that God can heal, but you've got to settle in your heart whether He is willing to heal you.

B. Jesus is the same yesterday, today, and forever. So, if it was God's will to heal every time when He walked the earth, then it must be His will today.

> *Jesus Christ is the same yesterday, today, and forever.*
>
> Hebrews 13:8

C. The devil is defeated, but he's not dead. The devil can only devour people who do not know the truth intimately and do not exercise their authority over him.

> *Be sober, be vigilant; because your adversary the devil walks about like a roaring lion, seeking whom he may devour.*
>
> 1 Peter 5:8

D. The Pharisees in that day and time had no problem with Jesus's ability to heal. It was His ability to forgive sins that they had a huge problem with.

And the scribes and the Pharisees began to reason, saying, "Who is this who speaks blasphemies? Who can forgive sins but God alone?" But when Jesus perceived their thoughts, He answered and said to them, "Why are you reasoning in your hearts? Which is easier, to say, 'Your sins are forgiven you,' or to say, 'Rise up and walk'? But that you may know that the Son of Man has power on earth to forgive sins"—He said to the man who was paralyzed, "I say to you, arise, take up your bed, and go to your house."

Luke 5:21–24

E. Which is easier, forgiveness or healing? Neither is easier because the same sacrifice paid for both. Jesus paid the price for everything that we need—healing and forgiveness of sins. One sacrifice paid for the entire package.

Which is easier, to say, "Your sins are forgiven you," or to say, "Rise up and walk"?

Luke 5:23

F. It's not sin that keeps you from healing; it's what you believe about Jesus.

Surely He has borne our griefs And carried our sorrows; Yet we esteemed Him stricken, Smitten by God, and afflicted.

Isaiah 53:4

II. You have the power, so use it.

Then He called His twelve disciples together and gave them power and authority over all demons, and to cure diseases. He sent them to preach the kingdom of God and to heal the sick.

Luke 9:1–2

A. The word here "power" is the Greek word *dunamis*, which means miraculous power, force, or might. It means the ability to make possible. "Authority" used here is the Greek word *exousia*, and it means privilege, authority, capacity, competency, control, and jurisdiction.

B. Jesus said to all of His disciples, which includes you and me, that He gave us the *dunamis* power—miraculous power—to heal the sick. He also gave us the *exousia* power, which is the jurisdiction or the control.

C. Jesus has given you and me those same dimensions of power and authority. We've got the power, the *dunamis* power, the gifts of the Spirit, the Word of God, and the name of Jesus. Yet, many times we pick up our prayer phone line and we call Jesus and ask, "Lord, would You come and get rid of the devil for me?"

D. This *dunamis* power He has given us is released whenever we exercise the *exousia* power.

E. The power of the Lord is released whenever you and I exercise it, operate in it, and run the enemy out of our bodies.

F. Jesus has given us the jurisdiction, the control, the authority, the power of the Word, and the gifts of the Spirit to stop the works of the enemy. We have that power, and we've got to use it. We need to stop praying for God to do something that He has delegated us to do.

And I will give you the keys of the kingdom of heaven, and whatever you bind on earth will be bound in heaven, and whatever you loose on earth will be loosed in heaven.

Matthew 16:19

G. We need to get angry at the enemy, and we need to run him out of our lives. You and I have that authority, and we need to operate in it.

H. The centurion understood that Jesus had authority over sickness and disease. The centurion reasoned from his own experience with authority that Jesus could simply use His Word to command sickness and disease to leave the centurion's servant who was sick without coming to his house.

Now when Jesus had entered Capernaum, a centurion came to Him, pleading with Him, saying, "Lord, my servant is lying at home paralyzed, dreadfully tormented." And Jesus said to him, "I will come and heal him." The centurion answered and said, "Lord, I am not worthy that You should come under my roof. But only speak a word, and my servant will be healed. For I also am a man under authority, having soldiers under me. And I say to this one, 'Go,' and he goes; and to another, 'Come,' and he comes; and to my servant, 'Do this,' and he does it."

Matthew 8:5–9

I. Since Jesus delegated His authority to us, we have the same power over sickness, disease, and pain that He had. His Word on our lips carries the same authority over these enemies today as it did with Jesus when He walked the earth.

III.   Keep exalting the truth above the facts until the truth prevails.

Who has believed our report? And to whom has the arm of the Lord been revealed?

Isaiah 53:1

A. The power of the Lord, including healing, is revealed to whoever believes His report in the Word of God above any other report.

B. I denied symptoms and reports to have final authority in my body. I exalted the truth of God's Word over the facts of what the doctors were saying to me.

C. You cannot resist a negative report while you're submitting to it.

D. The Word of God trumps every other report.

E. Your experience is temporal. God's Word is eternal.

F. What are you going to say about your situation? Your word is law in the spirit realm.

What then shall we say to these things? If God is for us, who can be against us?

Romans 8:31

G. People put all of their healing eggs in the instantaneous healing basket, but the truth is, recovery implies process. So, most healing is not instantaneous.

They will take up serpents; and if they drink anything deadly, it will by no means hurt them; they will lay hands on the sick, and they will recover.

Mark 16:18

H. You'll reap if you don't faint. Don't stop believing. Don't stop exalting the truth above the facts. Don't stop confessing the Word of God, and you will receive.

And let us not grow weary while doing good, for in due season we shall reap if we do not lose heart.

Galatians 6:9

LESSON REVIEW QUESTIONS

1. How do you know that healing is the will of God for everyone, all the time?

2. Explain *dunamis* power.

3. Explain *exousia* power.

4. To whom did Jesus give *dunamis* and *exousia* power?

5. How can you use *dunamis* and *exousia* power in your life?

6. What does it mean to exalt the truth above the facts?

1. How do you know that healing is the will of God for everyone, all the time?

    Possible answers: Jesus is the same yesterday, today, and forever, and He healed all; in the Atonement, Jesus paid the price for everything we need, including healing.

2. Explain *dunamis* power.

    Dunamis means miraculous power, force, or might, and the ability to make something possible. It is like a gun, taser, handcuffs or car that helps a deputy bring in a criminal.

3. Explain *exousia* power.

    ***Exousia* means privilege, authority, capacity, competency, control, and jurisdiction. It is like the badge of a deputy that gives him jurisdiction in a city or town to enforce the law with the complete backing of the entire police department.**

4. To whom did Jesus give *dunamis* and *exousia* power?

    He gave His disciples power and authority, and we are His disciples.

5. How can you use *dunamis* and *exousia* power in your life?

    I use *dunamis* power when I use the gifts of the Spirit, the Word of God, and the name of Jesus. I use exousia power when I exercise the authority to run sickness out of my body.

6. What does it mean to exalt the truth above the facts?

    Possible answers: I exalt the truth of God's Word over the facts of what the doctors say; I don't submit to a negative report, because God's Word trumps every report.

POINTS TO PONDER

- It really takes no faith to believe that God can heal, but you've got to settle in your heart if He is willing to heal.

- There are things that happen behind the scenes we don't see, or we don't know. We don't know what people believe, or what decisions they've made, but no matter what has happened, whether it seems like a faith failure or not, it doesn't change God's will to heal.

- Modern-day Pharisees, or the religious crowd, have no problem with the fact that our sins can be forgiven, but healing for anyone who asks it is a different story.

- People are approaching God for healing like they're approaching a loan officer for an unsecured loan. They don't realize the price has already been paid and it's already been deposited in their spiritual account.

- When you approach God for forgiveness, or when you lead someone to the Lord, you don't ever question that God would or would not forgive that person. However, if they don't see that healing has also been paid for in the Atonement, they won't have the same confidence to receive it as well.

- I refuse to carry or bear what Jesus died to free me from. The Atonement and finished work of the cross is a complete package.

- Not everyone receives salvation automatically—they have to believe. The same thing is true with healing.

- *Exousia* is like the badge of a deputy that gives him jurisdiction to enforce the law, and he has the backing of the entire police department. *Dunamis* is like the gun, the taser, the handcuffs, or the car that is used to bring criminals into jail to protect the citizens. The police chief is not going to do the job of the deputy. The chief of police is going to say, "I've given you authority, arrest him."

- You've got to drive the enemy, sickness, disease, and pain out of your body. The devil is a trespasser, and you have authority over him.

- Bob Nichols made this statement, "The first report is not the last report."

- Deny problems the right to have final authority in your life. Until you make God's Word the highest authority, it will not have complete authority in your life.

- I call my body, "Healingville." I've been given delegated authority, and delegated authority trumps functional authority. It has a higher value than the functional authority of a doctor.

- You've got to run doubt out, and you've got to stand your ground, even when the symptoms try to prevail. You've got to keep exalting the truth above the facts, and the truth will prevail.

- You cannot receive from God with your eyes on the calendar or on the clock.

- Every prayer of faith, every step of obedience, and every confession of the Word where you are exalting the truth above the facts is another swing of the sword of the Spirit that will eventually cut you completely free from sickness, disease, and pain.

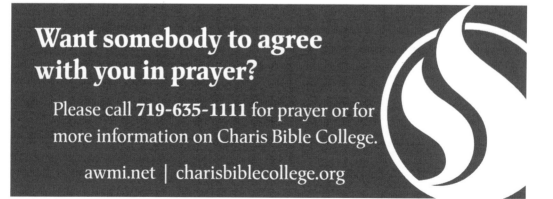

GO DEEPER

Self-Examination Questions

Do you believe healing is the will of God for everyone, every time, and all the time? Why or why not?

Have you ever thought, "If it's Gods will to heal every time, why am I struggling to receive my healing?" What answer do you have for this question now?

Can you think of an example of using your power and authority to speak to the enemy or sickness? Do you regularly use your power and authority in any area of your life, or does that need to change?

How will you exalt the truth above the facts of your health?

Prayer Points

Use these prayer points to write and to pray your own powerful prayer:

- Thank God for healing.
- Thank God that healing is His will for everyone, every time.
- Confess that you have not consistently used the power and authority He gave you.
- Praise Jesus for giving you *dunamis* and *exousia* power to use against sickness and the enemy.
- Proclaim that your focus will be on God's Word and not your condition or how long you've waited for healing.
- Declare the truth of God's Word over any facts about your health.

Action Steps

- In your Healing University journal, use the example of a deputy with a badge and weapon to draw a picture or write a scenario about your health. Imagine using your power and authority to confront your sickness, arrest it, and put it in a jail, out of your body. Draw or write what that looks like and what truth from God's Word you use to show your power and authority.

- Settle in your heart that healing is the will of God and that Jesus has given you the power and authority to stop the works of the enemy. Examine your heart and, when you are ready, make the following declaration and don't waver from it:

  I believe that healing is the will of God, and Jesus has given me the power and authority to stop the works of the enemy.

  _____ (sign and date)

- Write your own answer to this question: *How will you use your power and authority concerning your health?*

Need prayer?

Please call **719-635-1111** for prayer or for more information on Charis Bible College.

awmi.net | charisbiblecollege.org

SCRIPTURES

How God Heals Part 1

Luke 5:12–13

> And it happened when He was in a certain city, that behold, a man who was full of leprosy saw Jesus; and he fell on his face and implored Him, saying, "Lord, if You are willing, You can make me clean." Then He put out His hand and touched him, saying, "I am willing; be cleansed." Immediately the leprosy left him.

Hebrews 13:8

> Jesus Christ is the same yesterday, today, and forever.

1 Peter 5:8

> Be sober, be vigilant; because your adversary the devil walks about like a roaring lion, seeking whom he may devour.

Luke 5:17

> Now it happened on a certain day, as He was teaching, that there were Pharisees and teachers of the law sitting by, who had come out of every town of Galilee, Judea, and Jerusalem. And the power of the Lord was present to heal them.

Luke 5:18–20

> Then behold, men brought on a bed a man who was paralyzed, whom they sought to bring in and lay before Him. And when they could not find how they might bring him in, because of the crowd, they went up on the housetop and let him down with his bed through the tiling into the midst before Jesus. When He saw their faith, He said to him, "Man, your sins are forgiven you."

Luke 5:21–24

> And the scribes and the Pharisees began to reason, saying, "Who is this who speaks blasphemies? Who can forgive sins but God alone?" But when Jesus perceived their thoughts, He answered and said to them, "Why are you reasoning in your hearts? Which is easier, to say, 'Your sins are forgiven you,' or to say, 'Rise up and walk'? But that you may know that the Son of Man has power on earth to forgive sins"—

He said to the man who was paralyzed, "I say to you, arise, take up your bed, and go to your house."

Matthew 8:16–17

When evening had come, they brought to Him many who were demon-possessed. And He cast out the spirits with a word, and healed all who were sick, that it might be fulfilled which was spoken by Isaiah the prophet, saying: "He Himself took our infirmities And bore our sicknesses."

Isaiah 53:4–5

Surely He has borne our griefs And carried our sorrows; Yet we esteemed Him stricken, Smitten by God, and afflicted. But He was wounded for our transgressions, He was bruised for our iniquities; The chastisement for our peace was upon Him, And by His stripes we are healed.

Luke 9:1–2

Then He called His twelve disciples together and gave them power and authority over all demons, and to cure diseases. He sent them to preach the kingdom of God and to heal the sick.

Matthew 10:8

Heal the sick, cleanse the lepers, raise the dead, cast out demons. Freely you have received, freely give.

Matthew 16:19

And I will give you the keys of the kingdom of heaven, and whatever you bind on earth will be bound in heaven, and whatever you loose on earth will be loosed in heaven.

Matthew 8:5–9

Now when Jesus had entered Capernaum, a centurion came to Him, pleading with Him, saying, "Lord, my servant is lying at home paralyzed, dreadfully tormented." And Jesus said to him, "I will come and heal him." The centurion answered and said, "Lord, I am not worthy that You should come under my roof. But only speak a word, and my servant will be healed. For I also am a man under authority, having soldiers under me. And I say to this one, 'Go,' and he goes; and to another, 'Come,' and he comes; and to my servant, 'Do this,' and he does it."

Matthew 8:10–13

> When Jesus heard it, He marveled, and said to those who followed, "Assuredly, I say to you, I have not found such great faith, not even in Israel! And I say to you that many will come from east and west, and sit down with Abraham, Isaac, and Jacob in the kingdom of heaven. But the sons of the kingdom will be cast out into outer darkness. There will be weeping and gnashing of teeth." Then Jesus said to the centurion, "Go your way; and as you have believed, so let it be done for you." And his servant was healed that same hour.

Isaiah 53:1

> Who has believed our report? And to whom has the arm of the Lord been revealed?

1 Peter 2:24

> Who Himself bore our sins in His own body on the tree, that we, having died to sins, might live for righteousness—by whose stripes you were healed.

James 4:7

> Therefore submit to God. Resist the devil and he will flee from you.

Romans 8:31

> What then shall we say to these things? If God is for us, who can be against us?

Mark 16:18

> They will take up serpents; and if they drink anything deadly, it will by no means hurt them; they will lay hands on the sick, and they will recover.

Galatians 6:9

> And let us not grow weary while doing good, for in due season we shall reap if we do not lose heart.

Mark 5:25–34

> Now a certain woman had a flow of blood for twelve years, and had suffered many things from many physicians. She had spent all that she had and was no better, but rather grew worse. When she heard about Jesus, she came behind Him in the crowd and touched His garment. For she said, "If only I may touch His clothes, I shall be made well." Immediately the fountain of her blood was dried up, and she felt in her body that she was healed of the affliction. And Jesus, immediately knowing in Himself that power had gone out of Him, turned around in the crowd and said, "Who

touched My clothes?" But His disciples said to Him, "You see the multitude thronging You, and You say, 'Who touched Me?'" And He looked around to see her who had done this thing. But the woman, fearing and trembling, knowing what had happened to her, came and fell down before Him and told Him the whole truth. And He said to her, "Daughter, your faith has made you well. Go in peace, and be healed of your affliction."

Luke 8:43–48

Now a woman, having a flow of blood for twelve years, who had spent all her livelihood on physicians and could not be healed by any, came from behind and touched the border of His garment. And immediately her flow of blood stopped. And Jesus said, "Who touched Me?" When all denied it, Peter and those with him said, "Master, the multitudes throng and press You, and You say, 'Who touched Me?'" But Jesus said, "Somebody touched Me, for I perceived power going out from Me." Now when the woman saw that she was not hidden, she came trembling; and falling down before Him, she declared to Him in the presence of all the people the reason she had touched Him and how she was healed immediately. And He said to her, "Daughter, be of good cheer; your faith has made you well. Go in peace."

Acts 3:2–8

And a certain man lame from his mother's womb was carried, whom they laid daily at the gate of the temple which is called Beautiful, to ask alms from those who entered the temple; who, seeing Peter and John about to go into the temple, asked for alms. And fixing his eyes on him, with John, Peter said, "Look at us." So he gave them his attention, expecting to receive something from them. Then Peter said, "Silver and gold I do not have, but what I do have I give you: In the name of Jesus Christ of Nazareth, rise up and walk." And he took him by the right hand and lifted him up, and immediately his feet and ankle bones received strength. So he, leaping up, stood and walked and entered the temple with them—walking, leaping, and praising God.

Lesson 13
How God Heals Part 2
Instructor
Greg Mohr

VIDEO OUTLINE

Note: All scriptures used in this lesson are quoted from the *New King James Version*.

I.   There are many ways to receive healing. God always heals, but He doesn't always use the same method. It only takes one key of revelation to unlock a healing door for you.

   A. Know that healing is the will of God for everyone, every time, all the time.

   B. You have the power of God, so use it. You've got authority.

   C. Keep exalting the truth above the facts until the truth prevails.

II.   A key that will help you receive healing is to understand that you're loved. Faith works best when we understand we're loved.

   For in Christ Jesus neither circumcision nor uncircumcision avails anything, but faith working through love.

   Galatians 5:6

   A. I said, "Lord, don't let my ignorance stop the healing power of God from manifesting in my baby. This is my baby. I know you healed all those others, but Lord I need your healing power to manifest here in my house."

   B. God loves you. God will meet you where you are. And too many times, what happens—especially where our children are concerned—is we get desperate.

   C. Focus on the Lord, and let Him reveal to you how much He loves and cares for you.

   D. There's nothing you've done in life, no mistake you've made, that's going to keep God's love from extending to you.

   E. God's love is superabundant, and He's not holding out on you. He's not holding back from you.

[That you] may be able to comprehend with all the saints what is the width and length and depth and height—to know the love of Christ which passes knowledge; that you may be filled with all the fullness of God.

Ephesians 3:18–19

F. If you love your children, where did you get that love? You got it from your heavenly Father. Your Father gave you the ability to love, and how much more will God's love for His children cause healing to come?

If you then, being evil, know how to give good gifts to your children, how much more will your Father who is in heaven give good things to those who ask Him!

Matthew 7:11

G. The doctor said this, and the doctor said that. God's love and His Word is greater than what the doctors say. He loves you.

III. Once you meditate on God's love for you, then you will be able to see yourself well.

A. Once a different picture than the truth is planted in your heart, it's difficult to believe the Word of God in that area of your life.

B. Let the Word of God and the Spirit of God erase the picture of you being sick.

C. We've got to change our focus until we see ourselves well on the inside. We become like whatever we behold.

But we all, with unveiled face, beholding as in a mirror the glory of the Lord, are being transformed into the same image from glory to glory, just as by the Spirit of the Lord.

2 Corinthians 3:18

D. Hear the Word and focus on the Word. It's not just one time that you hear the Word—it's hearing and hearing.

So then faith comes by hearing, and hearing by the word of God.

Romans 10:17

E. The attention factor: get your attention off the pain, off the doctor's report, and focus on the Lord so that the picture on the inside will change.

My son, give attention to my words; Incline your ear to my sayings. Do not let them depart from your eyes; Keep them in the midst of your heart; For they are life to those who find them, And health to all their flesh.

Proverbs 4:20–22

F. Your soul—your mind, will, and emotions—is a magnifier. Whatever your soul magnifies will determine either the releasing or the binding of what God has placed and deposited in your spirit.

And Mary said: "My soul magnifies the Lord, And my spirit has rejoiced in God my Savior."

Luke 1:46–47

G. The soul of the Israelite people was much discouraged because they had forgotten the miracles that God did for them. They got their eyes off of God. They got their eyes on the condition of the way. We cannot afford to let the barometer of our soul rise and fall based upon the condition of the way (our path) or the condition of our bodies.

Then they journeyed from Mount Hor by the Way of the Red Sea, to go around the land of Edom; and the soul of the people became very discouraged on the way.

Numbers 21:4

H. God told Moses to put a fiery serpent on a pole, which was a type of Jesus who was to come, who would take all of our sicknesses and diseases upon Himself on the cross. He said whoever looks, beholds, inspects, and considers that sacrifice of Jesus to come would live. Whoever changes his focus from the condition of the way to the Maker of the way will live.

And as Moses lifted up the serpent in the wilderness, even so must the Son of Man be lifted up.

John 3:14

IV. Another principle is dealing with counterattacks. More battles are lost in counterattacks than in any other kind of battle.

A. Demons can't find rest outside of bodies. Jesus said that there is a demon that calls your body his house. Spirits of infirmity, iniquity, and uncleanness say, "Well, I'm going to return to my house." There's a demon who calls your body his house. Don't give the devil any room.

> *When an unclean spirit goes out of a man, he goes through dry places, seeking rest, and finds none. Then he says, "I will return to my house from which I came." And when he comes, he finds it empty, swept, and put in order. Then he goes and takes with him seven other spirits more wicked than himself, and they enter and dwell there; and the last state of that man is worse than the first. So shall it also be with this wicked generation.*
>
> Matthew 12:43–45

B. Understanding this truth prepares us for future attacks. We were ready for the counterattack, and you need to be ready as well. Don't be naïve, and don't let your spiritual guard down.

C. When you're ready for these counterattacks and you run the enemy off with the Word, it puts fear in him about trying to attack you again. He'll think twice about coming to your house to try to steal from you.

> *But He answered and said, "It is written, 'Man shall not live by bread alone, but by every word that proceeds from the mouth of God.'"*
>
> *Jesus said to him, "It is written again, 'You shall not tempt the Lord your God.'"*
>
> *Then Jesus said to him, "Away with you, Satan! For it is written, 'You shall worship the Lord your God, and Him only you shall serve.'"*
>
> Matthew 4:4, 7, and 10

D. If you consistently resist the devil with the Word, he will flee.

> *Therefore submit to God. Resist the devil and he will flee from you.*
>
> James 4:7

E. Some people who are healed through the gifts of the Spirit lose their healing later because they've not taken the time after receiving their healing to get filled with the Word of God.

F. God laughs at the devil, and the devil doesn't know what to do when you laugh at him. When he comes back to try to take from you, just start laughing at him.

He who sits in the heavens shall laugh; The Lord shall hold them in derision.

Psalms 2:4

G. Stay in faith. Be ready for the devil's counterattacks, and you won't be defeated by them. Stay in faith in the Word regarding every aspect of your being. Don't doubt your healing when the devil comes cloaked in a pain or another lying symptom of sickness or disease.

1. Why is it important to believe that God loves you?

2. What does 2 Corinthians 3:18 remind us to do concerning our health?

3. How can you change the vision in your heart?

4. Use John 3:14 to explain how the Israelites changed their focus.

5. Why do some people lose their healing?

6. How can you address lying symptoms and other counterattacks?

Want somebody to agree with you in prayer?

Please call **719-635-1111** for prayer or for more information on Charis Bible College.

awmi.net | charisbiblecollege.org

**LESSON REVIEW
ANSWERS**

1. Why is it important to believe that God loves you?

    Possible answers: Faith rises up when I know I'm loved by God; God's love is like a parent's love for their child, and parents want their children healed.

2. What does 2 Corinthians 3:18 remind us to do concerning our health?

    We become like what we behold. We need to begin to see ourselves as healed on the inside.

3. How can you change the vision in your heart?

    Focus on the Word of God to produce faith that changes the vision of the heart.

4. Use John 3:14 to explain how the Israelites changed their focus.

    Possible answer: The Israelites were discouraged and murmured, so God told Moses to make a fiery snake on a pole. In order to live, the Israelites had to look up at the pole and see a type of Jesus who would come and heal. They had to get their eyes off their problems.

5. Why do some people lose their healing?

    Possible answers: Some people lose their healing because they were healed by gifts of the Spirit but don't have the Word of God inside them to guard the healing from counterattacks; they might not focus on keeping a picture on the inside of themselves healed; they doubted.

6. How can you address lying symptoms and other counterattacks?

    I need to get the Word of God on the inside of me and speak God's Word to the symptoms and the devil.

POINTS TO PONDER

- Faith works in our lives when we understand we're loved.

- F. F. Bosworth, who wrote *Christ the Healer* says, "It's not what God can do, but what we know He yearns to do that inspires faith."

- Take a chill pill and rest in the fact that God loves you. He cares about you. He wants your child healed. He wants you healed. He loves you. He has compassion for you, and He's already provided healing for you. If there is anything you need to know, if there is anything you need to do, the Lord's going to show it to you.

- God's no respecter of persons. He's not going to get healing to you because you know you're some super-duper person, or you live right, or you do everything right. He loves you. You're His child.

- Ken Blue, who wrote *The Authority to Heal*, said, "Saturating our minds with the truth of God's unconditional love will do more to create a healing environment than anything else we can do."

- Focus on the scriptures that talk about God's love for you; it is a boost to your faith.

- Your body will line up with whatever picture you have on the inside.

- God said, "I don't want you to trust in a principle that I led you to do the last time you received from Me. I want you to look to Me, and I'll show you if there is anything you need to do."

- If you'll focus on the Lord and on His Word, your vision will change.

- Get your focus in the right place through giving attention to the Word, and the King of Glory, who's already on the inside of you, will manifest in your soul and physical body.

- Whoever will behold, inspect, perceive, and consider what Jesus has accomplished through the finished work of the cross will live.

- Get your eyes off the calendar or the clock. Get your eyes off of the pain, the sickness and disease, and how long it's been. Get your eyes off of the condition of the way and get your focus on the Maker of the way. The Maker of the way will change the condition of your way.

- Once you experience a spiritual victory and receive your healing, the devil will be back. That's not to fear. You need to understand. You need to be ready for him. He's a creature of pride, and whenever he comes and you defeat him with the Word, he will think twice about coming back to your house. He's after the Word. Don't let the Word go. When he comes to steal it, stick him with it.

- If the devil knocks on your door, let faith, Jesus, and the Word of God answer him. "It is written, by His stripes I'm healed. It is written, I've got authority over you. I rebuke you!" Then watch him flee.

- In his book, *How to Keep Your Healing*, Kenneth Hagin wrote, "Yes, the devil will try to put things back on you. But if the Word of God has been built into your heart, if you've meditated upon it long enough, fed on it, put it into your heart until you know it's become a part of you, your inner consciousness, you can put the devil on the run every time. If temptation comes, if pain comes, instead of being afraid and panicking and submitting to that, just start laughing, ha-ha, ha-ha, ha-ha."

GO DEEPER

Self–Examination Questions

What is God saying to you about how you will be healed?

What scriptures are you standing on and speaking out?

What picture do you have on the inside of you about your health?

How are you preparing in advance for counterattacks from the devil?

Prayer Points

Use these prayer points to write and to pray your own powerful prayer:

- Thank God that you are a victor and not a victim.
- Thank God that you are His beloved and He loves you.
- Ask God to continue to reveal to you how loved you are by Him.
- Ask God to give you courage to focus and change focus from the condition of the way to the Maker of the way.
- Thank God for providing His Word to use against counterattacks.
- Proclaim that you will prepare and fill yourself with the Word of God.
- Praise God that His love and His Word makes you whole.

Action Steps

- In your Healing University journal, write down a preparedness guide of how you will deal with counterattacks to your healing. Be specific. As you research and write down verses, make a plan for when and how you will use those verses. For example, make a recording of the scriptures and continually play it. Memorize them, put them on index cards on a ring, and read through them each night before bedtime.

- Settle in your heart that God loves you and wants you to see yourself healed. God wants you to get the Word inside you to prepare you to keep your healing. Examine your heart and, when you are ready, make the following declaration and don't waver from it:

I believe God loves me and wants me to see myself healed. I will begin to get the Word of God inside me to prepare to keep my healing during counterattacks.

_____ (sign and date)

- Write your own answer to this question: *How will you prepare to keep your healing?*

How God Heals Part 2

Philippians 1:23–24

For I am hard-pressed between the two, having a desire to depart and be with Christ, which is far better. Nevertheless to remain in the flesh is more needful for you.

Psalms 91:16

With long life I will satisfy him, And show him My salvation.

2 Peter 3:9

The Lord is not slack concerning His promise, as some count slackness, but is long-suffering toward us, not willing that any should perish but that all should come to repentance.

2 Peter 3:15

And consider that the longsuffering of our Lord is salvation—as also our beloved brother Paul, according to the wisdom given to him, has written to you.

Galatians 5:6

For in Christ Jesus neither circumcision nor uncircumcision avails anything, but faith working through love.

Ephesians 3:18–19

May be able to comprehend with all the saints what is the width and length and depth and height—to know the love of Christ which passes knowledge; that you may be filled with all the fullness of God.

Acts 10:34

Then Peter opened his mouth and said: "In truth I perceive that God shows no partiality."

Romans 2:11

For there is no partiality with God.

Matthew 7:11

If you then, being evil, know how to give good gifts to your children, how much more will your Father who is in heaven give good things to those who ask Him!

2 Corinthians 5:21

For He made Him who knew no sin to be sin for us, that we might become the righteousness of God in Him.

2 Corinthians 3:18

But we all, with unveiled face, beholding as in a mirror the glory of the Lord, are being transformed into the same image from glory to glory, just as by the Spirit of the Lord.

Romans 10:17

So then faith comes by hearing, and hearing by the word of God.

Proverbs 4:20–22

My son, give attention to my words; Incline your ear to my sayings. Do not let them depart from your eyes; Keep them in the midst of your heart; For they are life to those who find them, And health to all their flesh.

Psalms 119:89–90

Forever, O Lord, Your word is settled in heaven. Your faithfulness endures to all generations; You established the earth, and it abides.

Luke 1:46–47

And Mary said: "My soul magnifies the Lord, And my spirit has rejoiced in God my Savior…"

Psalm 24:7

Lift up your heads, O you gates! And be lifted up, you everlasting doors! And the King of glory shall come in.

Revelation 3:20

Behold, I stand at the door and knock. If anyone hears My voice and opens the door, I will come in to him and dine with him, and he with Me.

Numbers 21:1–4

The king of Arad, the Canaanite, who dwelt in the South, heard that Israel was coming on the road to Atharim. Then he fought against Israel and took some of them prisoners. So Israel made a vow to the Lord, and said, "If You will indeed deliver this people into my hand, then I will utterly destroy their cities." And the Lord listened to the voice of Israel and delivered up the Canaanites, and they utterly destroyed them and their cities. So the name of that place was called Hormah. Then they journeyed from Mount Hor by the Way of the Red Sea, to go around the land of Edom; and the soul of the people became very discouraged on the way.

John 3:14

And as Moses lifted up the serpent in the wilderness, even so must the Son of Man be lifted up.

Matthew 12:43–45

When an unclean spirit goes out of a man, he goes through dry places, seeking rest, and finds none. Then he says, "I will return to my house from which I came." And when he comes, he finds it empty, swept, and put in order. Then he goes and takes with him seven other spirits more wicked than himself, and they enter and dwell there; and the last state of that man is worse than the first. So shall it also be with this wicked generation.

John 8:36

Therefore if the Son makes you free, you shall be free indeed.

1 Corinthians 6:19

Or do you not know that your body is the temple of the Holy Spirit who is in you, whom you have from God, and you are not your own?

Matthew 4:4, 7, and 10

But He answered and said, "It is written, 'Man shall not live by bread alone, but by every word that proceeds from the mouth of God.'"

Jesus said to him, "It is written again, 'You shall not tempt the Lord your God.'"

Then Jesus said to him, "Away with you, Satan! For it is written, 'You shall worship the Lord your God, and Him only you shall serve.'"

James 4:7

Therefore submit to God. Resist the devil and he will flee from you.

Psalms 2:4

He who sits in the heavens shall laugh; The Lord shall hold them in derision.

1 Peter 5:8–9

Be sober, be vigilant; because your adversary the devil walks about like a roaring lion, seeking whom he may devour. Resist him, steadfast in the faith, knowing that the same sufferings are experienced by your brotherhood in the world.

Jeremiah 31:3

The Lord has appeared of old to me, saying: "Yes, I have loved you with an everlasting love; Therefore with lovingkindness I have drawn you."

Romans 8:11

But if the Spirit of Him who raised Jesus from the dead dwells in you, He who raised Christ from the dead will also give life to your mortal bodies through His Spirit who dwells in you.

Romans 8:37

Yet in all these things we are more than conquerors through Him who loved us.

Lesson 14
The Authority of the Believer
Instructor
Carrie Pickett

Note: All scriptures used in this lesson are quoted from the *New King James Version*.

I.   It's really hard to operate in authority as a believer if you don't know who your God is. If God can do whatever He wants with no accountability, then there's no authority that you can actually use as His child.

   A. God is God, but because He is so good, He says, "I'm going to show you who I am and make it clear so you won't be confused, and you can walk with confidence."

   B. If you don't know who God is, then you won't know how to discern when the devil is trying to tell you, "That must be God," when it's really him.

   C. If you don't know who God is, then you won't know your authority over the enemy.

   D. If the enemy can confuse you on who God really is and what He does, then you will never step into your real authority.

II.   God gave authority to mankind; He gave authority to Adam.

   Then God said, "Let Us make man in Our image, according to Our likeness; let them have dominion over the fish of the sea, over the birds of the air, and over the cattle, over all the earth and over every creeping thing that creeps on the earth."

   Then God blessed them, and God said to them, "Be fruitful and multiply; fill the earth and subdue it; have dominion over the fish of the sea, over the birds of the air, and over every living thing that moves on the earth."

   Genesis 1:26 and 28

   A. Adam and Eve surrendered their authority to the enemy on the earth. The enemy gained power to rule, reign, and deceive, and people believe his lies.

Now the serpent was more cunning than any beast of the field which the Lord God had made. And he said to the woman, "Has God indeed said, 'You shall not eat of every tree of the garden'?" And the woman said to the serpent, "We may eat the fruit of the trees of the garden; but of the fruit of the tree which is in the midst of the garden, God has said, 'You shall not eat it, nor shall you touch it, lest you die.'" Then the serpent said to the woman, "You will not surely die. For God knows that in the day you eat of it your eyes will be opened, and you will be like God, knowing good and evil." So when the woman saw that the tree was good for food, that it was pleasant to the eyes, and a tree desirable to make one wise, she took of its fruit and ate. She also gave to her husband with her, and he ate.

Genesis 3:1–6

B. Even in the midst of Adam and Eve making a mistake, God already began to prophesy of the coming of Jesus, what Jesus was going to do, and how He was going to crush the head of the enemy through the power of the cross.

Then the Lord God called to Adam and said to him, "Where are you?" So he said, "I heard Your voice in the garden, and I was afraid because I was naked; and I hid myself." And He said, "Who told you that you were naked? Have you eaten from the tree of which I commanded you that you should not eat?" Then the man said, "The woman whom You gave to be with me, she gave me of the tree, and I ate." And the Lord God said to the woman, "What is this you have done?" The woman said, "The serpent deceived me, and I ate." So the Lord God said to the serpent: "Because you have done this, You are cursed more than all cattle, And more than every beast of the field; On your belly you shall go, And you shall eat dust All the days of your life. And I will put enmity Between you and the woman, And between your seed and her Seed; He shall bruise your head, And you shall bruise His heel."

Genesis 3:9–15

III. The redemption story is so beautiful. We were saved from our sins, from the power of sin and death, and from the ability of the enemy to do whatever, whenever. Now we have the authority with which to respond to him.

A. Jesus told His disciples, "Because of Me, because of My work, because of My sacrifice, and because of My resurrection, this is what I'm giving to you. This is now the commission that I'm putting upon you."

And Jesus came and spoke to them, saying, "All authority has been given to Me in heaven and on earth. Go therefore and make disciples of all the nations, baptizing them in the name of the Father and of the Son and of the Holy Spirit, teaching them to observe all things that I have commanded you; and lo, I am with you always, even to the end of the age." Amen.

Matthew 28:18–20

B. Jesus gave us the ability to go out with His authority and to destroy the works of the devil.

C. Regarding all the rules, regulations, and laws, Jesus said, "I've taken and fulfilled all the requirements. My blood has cleansed all these requirements that you had to do to get right with God. I'm going to be the perfect sacrifice. I am taking it all."

And you, being dead in your trespasses and the uncircumcision of your flesh, He has made alive together with Him, having forgiven you all trespasses, having wiped out the handwriting of requirements that was against us, which was contrary to us. And He has taken it out of the way, having nailed it to the cross. Having disarmed principalities and powers, He made a public spectacle of them, triumphing over them in it.

Colossians 2:13–15

D. Now, as a child of God, you have that authority in you and can change your world.

E. The devil is actually a defeated foe, but he's trying to tell you that he's not. That's why he will roar such crazy attacks at us.

Therefore submit to God. Resist the devil and he will flee from you.

James 4:7

IV. The truth of who Jesus is and what Jesus did is greater than the things the enemy is trying to deceive you to live with. The enemy is trying to tell you that the doctor has the authority and education to proclaim a diagnosis over your life.

A. There should be an attitude of faith that starts to stir up inside of you. "I'm not going to believe what I see. I'm not going to believe what I feel. I'm just going to believe God's Word!"

B. People who do not know their authority do not understand the covenant in which they live. They don't realize they're not of the Old Covenant, when the enemy had the authority.

C. When you understand who you are in the Spirit, you will say, "I am a child of God. I'm of the kingdom of God. I have the righteousness of Christ Jesus. I have the victory of the cross in me, and that is my authority."

D. When a situation tries to come, you can start quoting the Word. "No, devil, you're telling me this, but God promised me this, and all the promises of God are yes, and now I'm saying 'Amen,' because of what Jesus did for me."

For the word of God is living and powerful, and sharper than any two-edged sword, piercing even to the division of soul and spirit, and of joints and marrow, and is a discerner of the thoughts and intents of the heart.

Hebrews 4:12

V. You are a magnificent temple of the Holy Spirit.

A. We are the temple carrying the kingdom of God. We are the temple that gets to be used: our hands, our feet, and our words. It's through this temple that the Spirit of God shines. The enemy tries to attack because he doesn't want you to shine; he knows the power of what you can accomplish in this world.

VI. Start speaking out the testimony of what God has done in your spirit and your soul. Declare that your temple is going to glorify God, and begin rebuking your symptoms and disease.

A. The enemy is like a roaring lion. It doesn't say he is a roaring lion. When a lion roars, it is supposed to paralyze the prey. This is exactly what the enemy's tactic is today in the spirit. He will roar cancer, a diagnosis, or pain at you, and he looks to see how you respond.

Be sober, be vigilant; because your adversary the devil walks about like a roaring lion, seeking whom he may devour. Resist him, steadfast in the faith, knowing that the same sufferings are experienced by your brotherhood in the world.

1 Peter 5:8–9

B. Your ability to walk in your authority truly comes from understanding, "God loves me, I'm a new creation in the spirit, and as He is, so am I in this world. That means in this world I have the ability to walk in divine health, divine wisdom, and divine guidance because His Spirit lives within me. I can live in this world differently than those of the world."

VII. I don't care what has been declared over your life. I don't care what sickness people say is impossible to heal. Nothing is impossible to God, because in His Word He gave us truth, promises, and His covenant. He said, "This is the authority that I won back for you, and now I give it to you. And no matter what the enemy tries to tell you, he does not have any authority."

A. Speak your authority over the enemy. This is your weapon to resist the devil, and the Word says that he will flee.

LESSON REVIEW QUESTIONS

1. Why is it important for believers to understand they have authority?

2. Use Genesis 1 and Genesis 3 to explain how God-given authority changed hands.

3. How did Satan lose authority?

4. What does the Great Commission have to do with believers today (Matt. 28:19–20, Mark 16:15–18, Luke 24:46–49, and John 21:16–18)?

5. How can believers use their authority to make disciples?

6. According to 1 Peter 5:8–9, is Satan powerful enough to devour you?

7. What are some examples of taking your authority over sickness, such as during flu season?

Need prayer?

Please call **719-635-1111** for prayer or for more information on Charis Bible College.

awmi.net | charisbiblecollege.org

**LESSON REVIEW
ANSWERS**

1. Why is it important for believers to understand they have authority?

   Possible answer: If believers don't know their authority, they will submit to lies and sicknesses that they have power to rebuke; when believers know and use their authority, they can change the world.

2. Use Genesis 1 and Genesis 3 to explain how God-given authority changed hands.

   Genesis 1 explains that God gave mankind authority. Genesis 3 explains that Adam and Eve's sin transferred that authority to Satan.

3. How did Satan lose authority?

   Satan lost authority when Jesus won it back for us through His death on the cross and His resurrection.

4. What does the Great Commission have to do with believers today and healing (Matt. 28:19–20, Mark 16:15–18, Luke 24:46–49, and John 21:16–18)?

   Possible answer: Jesus won back all authority and gave it to His followers to use against the enemy and to go into all of the world and make disciples. We use that authority in all areas of our lives, including health. We can go make disciples and lay hands on the sick and they will recover.

5. How can believers use their authority to make disciples?

   Possible answers: Believers can help people understand what lies the enemy has told them and rebuke the lies so the people can see God's love for them; believers can use their authority to do signs and wonders to show God's power.

6. According to 1 Peter 5:8–9, is Satan powerful enough to devour you?

   No; Satan cannot devour me as long as I understand my authority and use it to rebuke him. Satan is like a roaring lion looking to devour, but I have authority to stop him and not fall for his lies.

7.   What are some examples of taking your authority over sickness, such as during flu season?

Answers will vary.

POINTS TO PONDER

- God puts Himself in the Word so that you can open it up and see how God will react. This is God's heart. This is what the kingdom of God looks like. If you know what the kingdom of God looks like, then you'll be able to discern and define what the kingdom of darkness looks like.

- When you know your authority, then you can look at sickness and say, "This is not the kingdom of God, this is not God's heart for me, this is not the goodness of God for me. I can clearly define and discern that this sickness and this attack is from the enemy. This lie does not match up with the truth and the goodness of this Word, and so I rebuke it."

- Jesus was born of a virgin, and He came as a man. He lived as a sinless man so that He could tell the enemy, "I did not believe your lies. Now My perfect death and resurrection takes back the authority, and now I have all authority on heaven and earth." Then He looked at you and I and said, "By the way, with this authority, I commission you to go out."

- Jesus took captivity captive and said, "Listen, the devil is a defeated foe in your life." And then He looked at you and me and said, "Listen, all authority has been given to Me, not the devil."

- The enemy may try to come against you, and he will try to convince you that he still has authority. Even though he's a defeated foe, he will still try to throw attacks and symptoms at you. He'll still try to do things to tell you he still has the authority so that you back down and cower in a corner.

- You can see the activity of the lies of the enemy in your body, in your family, in your marriage, and all these different things. But you've got to come to a place where what you see and what you feel isn't real to you; it's not the truth. The truth is that the enemy is a defeated foe.

- The truth is that your body is under the ownership of Jesus Christ. Because of what He did for you, because His Spirit lives within you, because the nature of Jehovah Rapha the Healer lives within you, you can live in the truth that is greater than your feelings.

- Renew your thinking so that when symptoms, sickness, diagnosis, debt, or relational issues try to come against you—saying that they have authority to define the quality and the longevity of your life—you will recognize that they are lies. When you put life inside of you, it will change the way you think, so when the enemy, or someone else, says something that doesn't match up with God's Word, you know it is not truth.

- Your temple is precious in the sight of God. God wants you not just to have life in your spirit, but abundant life to spill out into your whole being: your mind, your will, your emotions, and your body. This way—spirit, soul, and body—you will proclaim the glory and the goodness of God.

- You may be surrounded by sickness, but you don't have to get sick, because you believe that the Spirit of God and the authority in you is greater than anything else.

GO DEEPER

Self-Examination Questions

What lies about your authority as a believer have you believed? What truths will replace those lies?

What areas of your life do you need to take authority over? What will you do and say to establish that authority?

On a scale from 1–10 (low to high), how willing are you to use your authority from Christ to rebuke the enemy?

Prayer Points

Use these prayer points to write and to pray your own powerful prayer:

- Thank God for His goodness and love for you.
- Thank Jesus for winning back the authority that Adam and Eve gave to Satan.
- Praise Jesus for giving His authority to His followers.
- Thank God that He has given you authority to resist the devil and the promise that he will flee.
- Ask God to help you boldly take your authority and rebuke the enemy and his lies.
- Praise God that your body is the temple in which the Holy Spirit dwells.
- Thank God that His Spirit shines through your body, because you take authority over any lies or attacks against you.
- Thank Jesus for the victories you will have as you use your authority as a believer.

Action Steps

- In your Healing University journal, write out statements about who you are in Christ and what authority you have through the accomplished work of the cross. Now write down some of the lies that you've believed. Take a red pen, and over top of each lie write a rebuke explaining your authority and how you're using it against that lie.

- Settle in your heart that Jesus has all authority because of His victory on the cross and has given His authority to you to use against the lies of the enemy. Examine your heart and, when you are ready, make the following declaration and don't waver from it:

I believe that Jesus has all authority because of His victory on the cross and has given His authority to me to use against the lies of the enemy.

_____ (sign and date)

- Write your own answer to this question: *What is the authority of the believer?*

The Authority of the Believer

John 10:10

The thief does not come except to steal, and to kill, and to destroy. I have come that they may have life, and that they may have it more abundantly.

Jeremiah 29:11

For I know the thoughts that I think toward you, says the Lord, thoughts of peace and not of evil, to give you a future and a hope.

Genesis 1:26 and 28

Then God said, "Let Us make man in Our image, according to Our likeness; let them have dominion over the fish of the sea, over the birds of the air, and over the cattle, over all the earth and over every creeping thing that creeps on the earth."

Then God blessed them, and God said to them, "Be fruitful and multiply; fill the earth and subdue it; have dominion over the fish of the sea, over the birds of the air, and over every living thing that moves on the earth."

Genesis 3:1–6

Now the serpent was more cunning than any beast of the field which the Lord God had made. And he said to the woman, "Has God indeed said, 'You shall not eat of every tree of the garden'?" And the woman said to the serpent, "We may eat the fruit of the trees of the garden; but of the fruit of the tree which is in the midst of the garden, God has said, 'You shall not eat it, nor shall you touch it, lest you die.'" Then the serpent said to the woman, "You will not surely die. For God knows that in the day you eat of it your eyes will be opened, and you will be like God, knowing good and evil." So when the woman saw that the tree was good for food, that it was pleasant to the eyes, and a tree desirable to make one wise, she took of its fruit and ate. She also gave to her husband with her, and he ate.

Genesis 3:9–15

Then the Lord God called to Adam and said to him, "Where are you?" So he said, "I heard Your voice in the garden, and I was afraid because I was naked; and I hid myself." And He said, "Who told you that you were naked? Have you eaten from the tree of which I commanded you that you should not eat?" Then the man said, "The woman whom You gave to be with me, she gave me of the tree, and I ate." And the Lord God said to the woman, "What is this you have done?" The woman said, "The serpent deceived me, and I ate." So the Lord God said to the serpent: "Because you have done this, You are cursed more than all cattle, And more than every beast of the field; On your belly you shall go, And you shall eat dust All the days of your life. And I will put enmity Between you and the woman, And between your seed and her Seed; He shall bruise your head, And you shall bruise His heel."

2 Peter 3:9

The Lord is not slack concerning His promise, as some count slackness, but is long-suffering toward us, not willing that any should perish but that all should come to repentance.

Matthew 28:18–20

And Jesus came and spoke to them, saying, "All authority has been given to Me in heaven and on earth. Go therefore and make disciples of all the nations, baptizing them in the name of the Father and of the Son and of the Holy Spirit, teaching them to observe all things that I have commanded you; and lo, I am with you always, even to the end of the age." Amen.

Mark 16:15–18

And He said to them, "Go into all the world and preach the gospel to every creature. He who believes and is baptized will be saved; but he who does not believe will be condemned. And these signs will follow those who believe: In My name they will cast out demons; they will speak with new tongues; they will take up serpents; and if they drink anything deadly, it will by no means hurt them; they will lay hands on the sick, and they will recover."

Luke 24:46–49

Then He said to them, "Thus it is written, and thus it was necessary for the Christ to suffer and to rise from the dead the third day, and that repentance and remission of sins should be preached in His name to all nations, beginning at Jerusalem. And you are witnesses of these things. Behold, I send the Promise of My Father upon you; but tarry in the city of Jerusalem until you are endued with power from on high."

John 21:16–18

He said to him again a second time, "Simon, son of Jonah, do you love Me?" He said to Him, "Yes, Lord; You know that I love You." He said to him, "Tend My sheep." He said to him the third time, "Simon, son of Jonah, do you love Me?" Peter was grieved *because He said to him the third time, "Do you love Me?" And he said to Him, "Lord, You know all things; You know that I love You." Jesus said to him, "Feed My sheep. Most assuredly, I say to you, when you were younger, you girded yourself and walked where you wished; but when you are old, you will stretch out your hands, and another will gird you and carry you where you do not wish."*

Colossians 2:13–15

And you, being dead in your trespasses and the uncircumcision of your flesh, He has made alive together with Him, having forgiven you all trespasses, having wiped out the handwriting of requirements that was against us, which was contrary to us. And He has taken it out of the way, having nailed it to the cross. Having disarmed principalities and powers, He made a public spectacle of them, triumphing over them in it.

Revelations 1:18

I am He who lives, and was dead, and behold, I am alive forevermore. Amen. And I have the keys of Hades and of Death.

Ephesians 4:8

Therefore He says: "When He ascended on high, He led captivity captive, And gave gifts to men."

James 4:7

Therefore submit to God. Resist the devil and he will flee from you.

1 Thessalonians 5:23

Now may the God of peace Himself sanctify you completely; and may your whole spirit, soul, and body be preserved blameless at the coming of our Lord Jesus Christ.

Hebrews 4:12

For the word of God is living and powerful, and sharper than any two-edged sword, piercing even to the division of soul and spirit, and of joints and marrow, and is a discerner of the thoughts and intents of the heart.

1 Peter 5:8–9

Be sober, be vigilant; because your adversary the devil walks about like a roaring lion, seeking whom he may devour. Resist him, steadfast in the faith, knowing that the same sufferings are experienced by your brotherhood in the world.

Matthew 10:7-8

> *And as you go, preach, saying, "The kingdom of heaven is at hand." Heal the sick, cleanse the lepers, raise the dead, cast out demons. Freely you have received, freely give.*

Lesson 15
The Lordship of Jesus
Instructor
Barry Bennett

Note: All scriptures used in this lesson are quoted from the *New King James Version*.

I. We will easily say, "Jesus is my Lord," but the reality is many of us are living with other lords. In other words, other things are ruling over our lives. We become slaves to that to which we submit.

> *Do you not know that to whom you present yourselves slaves to obey, you are that one's slaves whom you obey, whether of sin leading to death, or of obedience leading to righteousness?*
>
> Romans 6:16

A. Lordship is both theological and practical. The practical side is how you are living. Is Jesus the Lord of your life, or are other things the lord of your life?

B. We can submit to the lordship of chronic sickness. Many people believe God could heal them, but He might not. That's a false lord, because the decision to heal all has already been made.

> *After this there was a feast of the Jews, and Jesus went up to Jerusalem. Now there is in Jerusalem by the Sheep Gate a pool, which is called in Hebrew, Bethesda, having five porches. In these lay a great multitude of sick people, blind, lame, paralyzed, waiting for the moving of the water. For an angel went down at a certain time into the pool and stirred up the water; then whoever stepped in first, after the stirring of the water, was made well of whatever disease he had. Now a certain man was there who had an infirmity thirty-eight years. When Jesus saw him lying there, and knew that he already had been in that condition a long time, He said to him, "Do you want to be made well?" The sick man answered Him, "Sir, I have no man to put me into the pool when the water is stirred up; but while I am coming, another steps down before me." Jesus said to him, "Rise, take up your bed and walk." And immediately the man was made well, took up his bed, and walked. And that day was the Sabbath.*
>
> John 5:1–9

C. The paralyzed man submitted to the lordship of bad teaching, or a superstition, and those things defined his life.

D. The paralyzed man submitted to a wrong concept of God. He didn't know the Word, the promises of God, or God's covenant. He left healing up to other lords, and those lords dominated his life.

E. Anything that's limiting your life is a false lord.

II. There are examples in the Bible showing that the people who got healed were willing to break the lordship that had bound them.

A. The woman with an issue of blood was moved to break through their traditions and through the law in order to get to Jesus, touch Him, and receive healing, because she was unwilling to submit to the lordship of the law.

Now a certain woman had a flow of blood for twelve years, and had suffered many things from many physicians. She had spent all that she had and was no better, but rather grew worse. When she heard about Jesus, she came behind Him in the crowd and touched His garment. For she said, "If only I may touch His clothes, I shall be made well." Immediately the fountain of her blood was dried up, and she felt in her body that she was healed of the affliction. And Jesus, immediately knowing in Himself that power had gone out of Him, turned around in the crowd and said, "Who touched My clothes?" But His disciples said to Him, "You see the multitude thronging You, and You say, 'Who touched Me?'" And He looked around to see her who had done this thing. But the woman, fearing and trembling, knowing what had happened to her, came and fell down before Him and told Him the whole truth. And He said to her, "Daughter, your faith has made you well. Go in peace, and be healed of your affliction."

Mark 5:25–34

B. In the story of the paralytic on a cot, his friends were unwilling to submit to the lordship of politeness and etiquette.

And again He entered Capernaum after some days, and it was heard that He was in the house. Immediately many gathered together, so that there was no longer room to receive them, not even near the door. And He preached the word to them. Then they came to Him, bringing a paralytic who was carried by four men. And when they could not come near Him because of the crowd, they uncovered the roof where He was. So when they had broken through, they let down the bed on which the paralytic was lying. When Jesus saw their faith, He said to the paralytic, "Son, your sins are forgiven you." And some of the scribes were sitting there and reasoning in their hearts, "Why does this Man speak blasphemies like this? Who can forgive sins but God alone?" But immediately, when Jesus perceived in His spirit that they reasoned thus within themselves, He said to them, "Why do you reason about these things in your hearts? Which is easier, to say to the paralytic, 'Your sins are forgiven you,' or to say, 'Arise, take up your bed and walk'? But that you may know that the Son of Man has power on earth to forgive sins"—He said to the paralytic, "I say to you, arise, take up your bed, and go to your house." Immediately he arose, took up the bed, and went out in the presence of them all, so that all were amazed and glorified God, saying, "We never saw anything like this!"

Mark 2:1–12

C. In the story of blind Bartimaeus, he knew it was Jesus walking by and that this was his chance. He wasn't lorded over by people's opinions. Bartimaeus was a blind beggar who wore a garment that people could see from a distance that identified him as a beggar. However, he didn't submit to the lordship of being known as a blind beggar. He didn't submit to an identity that limited him.

Now they came to Jericho. As He went out of Jericho with His disciples and a great multitude, blind Bartimaeus, the son of Timaeus, sat by the road begging. And when he heard that it was Jesus of Nazareth, he began to cry out and say, "Jesus, Son of David, have mercy on me!" Then many warned him to be quiet; but he cried out all the more, "Son of David, have mercy on me!" So Jesus stood still and commanded him to be called. Then they called the blind man, saying to him, "Be of good cheer. Rise, He is calling you." And throwing aside his garment, he rose and came to Jesus. So Jesus answered and said to him, "What do you want Me to do for you?" The blind man said to Him, "Rabboni, that I may receive my sight." Then Jesus said to him, "Go your way; your faith has made you well." And immediately he received his sight and followed Jesus on the road.

Mark 10:46–52

D. In the culture of the time, Gentiles—or Canaanites—were considered dogs, and Gentile women were the dogs of the dogs. The Canaanite woman refused to submit to the lordship of being considered inferior because she was a Canaanite and a woman. She refused that, and Jesus even used the common language of the day, "Gentiles are dogs." Yet, that didn't stop her.

From there He arose and went to the region of Tyre and Sidon. And He entered a house and wanted no one to know it, but He could not be hidden. For a woman whose young daughter had an unclean spirit heard about Him, and she came and fell at His feet. The woman was a Greek, a Syro-Phoenician by birth, and she kept asking Him to cast the demon out of her daughter. But Jesus said to her, "Let the children be filled first, for it is not good to take the children's bread and throw it to the little dogs." And she answered and said to Him, "Yes, Lord, yet even the little dogs under the table eat from the children's crumbs." Then He said to her, "For this saying go your way; the demon has gone out of your daughter." And when she had come to her house, she found the demon gone out, and her daughter lying on the bed.

Mark 7:24–30

III. We need to start knocking down some of these things that are restricting our lives and stealing from us.

    A. We've got to determine what has authority in our lives—the vision and the promises of God or a bank account and doctor's report.

    B. You can't let fear or your past be your lord, or you will never accomplish God's purpose for your life.

IV. False lords can be knocked over and done away with, and the truth will set you free.

    A. Your heart might have different little lords enthroned in it, and sickness or the doctor's report might be one of them. If you have allowed limitations in your life based upon those little lords in your heart, you can knock them down.

For as he thinks in his heart, so is he. "Eat and drink!" he says to you, But his heart is not with you.

Proverbs 23:7

    B. You can decide that Jesus is your Lord, and Jesus is the Lord of health and healing. Just the recognition of this will start setting you free, and you'll start moving into a new dimension of faith. You'll have a new vision for your life of the potential that is out there, and you can be healed, be whole, and walk in health.

    C. Choose to not look at circumstances, the past, people's opinions, inconveniences, limitations, education, or physical appearance. Choose to look at the things that are not seen, or in this context, choose to look at the Lordship of Jesus Christ.

While we do not look at the things which are seen, but at the things which are not seen. For the things which are seen are temporary, but the things which are not seen are eternal.

2 Corinthians 4:18

V. Spiritual eyes choose to see the Lordship of Jesus, not the lordships of limitations.

    A. Let us lay aside every lord that we have allowed to influence and constrain and restrict our lives, and let us press on.

> *Therefore we also, since we are surrounded by so great a cloud of witnesses, let us lay aside every weight, and the sin which so easily ensnares us, and let us run with endurance the race that is set before us, looking unto Jesus, the author and finisher of our faith, who for the joy that was set before Him endured the cross, despising the shame, and has sat down at the right hand of the throne of God.*
>
> Hebrews 12:1-2

    B. Some of us aren't getting healed because we're not calling on the name of the Lord. We're allowing other lords to dictate how we live. Superstitions, bad teaching, people's opinions, family history, educational level, and other lords have stolen from the Lord. We need to make a choice now and decide, "Enough with all these other lords. I'm going to submit to the Lord, the One who died for me, the One who has provided healing for my body and a purpose for my life, praise God."

> *For "whoever calls on the name of the Lord shall be saved."*
>
> Romans 10:13

    C. Make a choice that Jesus is your Lord. Put that revelation on, let that truth set you free, and make no provision for any other lord.

VI. You tell your body what's up. "Jesus is Lord, I'm getting up today. Jesus is Lord, I'm going to take care of myself today. Jesus is Lord, whatever I couldn't do yesterday, I'm going to do it today because Jesus is Lord, praise God." Now, there might be some resistance, but you have the Greater One living within you, the Lord Jesus Christ.

> *Therefore if the Son makes you free, you shall be free indeed.*
>
> John 8:36

    A. People who give up don't know who their lord is.

> *That you do not become sluggish, but imitate those who through faith and patience inherit the promises.*
>
> Hebrews 6:12

VII. The Lordship of Christ will lift you up, heal you, and set you on your eternal course.

    A. God wants you to enjoy the same quality of life that He enjoys, and He's given us promises, not limitations, not fear—but faith that the Lordship of Jesus could set us free to walk out our full purpose in health and enjoy life.

As His divine power has given to us all things that pertain to life and godliness, through the knowledge of Him who called us by glory and virtue, by which have been given to us exceedingly great and precious promises, that through these you may be partakers of the divine nature, having escaped the corruption that is in the world through lust.

2 Peter 1:3–4

    B. We have been translated from the dominion of other lords into the dominion of the Lord Jesus Christ, and His lordship is all about you being completely whole, completely healthy, and completely full of God's purpose, God's joy, and God's peace.

He has delivered us from the power of darkness and conveyed us into the kingdom of the Son of His love.

Colossians 1:13

LESSON REVIEW QUESTIONS

1. What is false lordship?

2. How does Romans 6:16 relate to lordship?

3. What biblical examples show people who were healed because they did not submit to false lords?

4. What will remove a false lord that is hindering your health?

5. What kinds of choices can we make to establish the Lordship of Jesus in our lives?

6. How does Romans 10:13 relate to false lords?

7. What are some false lords that might hinder someone's healing?

1. What is false lordship?

   False lordship is anything you allow to define and limit your life.

2. How does Romans 6:16 relate to lordship?

   Romans 6:16 points out that who you present yourself to, or submit to, you become a slave to. So, if you submit to fear from a doctor's report, you are a slave to that fear.

3. What biblical examples show people who were healed because they did not submit to false lords?

   The woman with the issue of blood chose not to submit to the law that identified her as unclean and unworthy of being in public. The four men carrying their friend on a cot chose not to submit to the lordship of politeness and etiquette. Blind Bartimaeus chose not to submit to the lordship of inferiority and fear. The Canaanite woman refused to submit to the lordship of being considered inferior because she was a Canaanite and a women.

4. What will remove a false lord that is hindering your health?

   Possible answers: The Word of God is the truth and will set you free from false lords; recognize that Jesus is Lord, and Jesus is Lord of health and healing.

5. What kinds of choices can we make to establish the Lordship of Jesus in our lives?

   Possible answers: We can lay aside every weight and sin; we can make no provision for the flesh; we can choose to establish His Lordship through His promises.

6. How does Romans 10:13 relate to false lords?

   Romans 10:13 reminds us to stop allowing false lords to steal from us. We can choose to submit and call on the Lord Jesus who provided healing.

7. What are some false lords that might hinder someone's healing?

Answers will vary.

POINTS TO PONDER

- In life we have many influences to which we can submit ourselves, knowingly or unknowingly, and allow to limit our lives to a much smaller realm than what God had in mind for us.

- Whatever we bow the knee to, or whatever has major influence in our lives, defines and constrains or puts limitations on our lives. Those things have become our lords.

- The paralyzed man submitted to a superstition, or a lordship of bad teaching, but something was ruling over his concept of God and how healing does or doesn't take place. There are many Christians that have a lordship of bad teaching, and they don't believe God will heal them.

- When you let people come up to you and say, "No, you can't do that; that's not how it's done; we've never done it that way before; no, this will never happen this way," you allow those things to restrict you. You are allowing something to steal your potential, vision, and proactive decision-making process. You've allowed another lord to come in and take charge in that situation.

- In the story of blind Bartimaeus, the same people who were against him and were telling him to shut up two minutes before were all on his side when he disregarded their fake lordship. People are fickle, and you need to beware of allowing people's opinions to restrict the grace of God in your life.

- Many people in our society walk around with a chronic inferiority complex because of all of the things that society is telling us are important. The inferiority complex has become a lord in their life. In the case of the Gentile woman, she had every reason to feel inferior because of how the Jews viewed her, yet that lord was not an impediment for her.

- As long as we're willing to submit to other lords, the Lordship of Jesus is simply a theology; it's not real.

- Many times, the doctor can keep you alive until you can get a word from God and get healed, so I'm not against doctors. I believe a doctor can serve you, but the moment he becomes your lord, you're in a bad place. A doctor needs to be a servant and not a lord. Once he becomes your lord, once his word is the last word and you bow the knee to that word, you're going to harvest whatever it is he's declared.

- Lay aside the cares of the world, fear, people's opinions, your family history, and the doctor's report. Lay that all aside and run your race with endurance, submitted to the Lordship of Jesus.

- The price has been paid for you to stand in God's presence without guilt, condemnation, or fear. The price has also been paid for you to be healed. Jesus wants to be the Lord of your life; Jesus wants to be the Healer of your life.

GO DEEPER

Self–Examination Questions

Do you say that Jesus is Lord, yet the reality of your life is different? How will your life show that Jesus is truly Lord of your life?

What false lords have you submitted to and why? What will you do remove lordship from them?

On a scale from 1–10 (low to high), how willing are you to submit to Jesus and allow Him to be Lord of your life?

Prayer Points

Use these prayer points to write and to pray your own powerful prayer.

- Thank God for His Lordship.
- Ask God to reveal false lords you've submitted to that have hindered your healing.
- Reject the false lordships of limitations, fear, the past, people's opinions, or doctor's reports.
- Proclaim that you choose to live a life that shows Jesus is Lord of your life.
- Thank God for His Word, which has all of the answers you need to have a sound mind.
- Praise God that the Lordship of Christ will lift you up, heal you, and set you on your eternal course.
- Commit to using your spiritual eyes to submit to the Lordship of Jesus in your life.
- Commit to establishing in your heart and mind the Lordship of Jesus and His promises.
- Thank God that you've been delivered from the power of the lords of darkness, corruption, fear, loss, sickness, and poverty.
- Choose to live in the kingdom of the Lord Jesus Christ and the reality of His redemptive work.

Action Steps

- In your Healing University journal, make a list of the false lords that you've been allowing to usurp the Lordship of Jesus. Write a declaration renouncing each false lord.

Create an announcement proclaiming each area of your life that you are inviting Jesus to be Lord over. Now write down steps or actions that will prove that you are really living with Jesus as Lord in these areas and not just saying words.

- Settle in your heart and decide that Jesus is your Lord and Jesus is the Lord of health and healing. The price has been paid for you to be healed. Jesus wants to be the Lord of your life; Jesus wants to be the healer of your life. Examine your heart and, when you are ready, make the following declaration and don't waver from it:

I choose to make Jesus the Lord of my life and the Lord of my health.

_____ (sign and date)

- Write your own answer to this question: *Is Jesus Lord over your health?*

The Lordship of Jesus

Romans 6:16

Do you not know that to whom you present yourselves slaves to obey, you are that one's slaves whom you obey, whether of sin leading *to death, or of obedience* leading *to righteousness?*

John 5:1–9

After this there was a feast of the Jews, and Jesus went up to Jerusalem. 2 Now there is in Jerusalem by the Sheep Gate *a pool, which is called in Hebrew, Bethesda, having five porches. In these lay a great multitude of sick people, blind, lame, paralyzed, waiting for the moving of the water. For an angel went down at a certain time into the pool and stirred up the water; then whoever stepped in first, after the stirring of the water, was made well of whatever disease he had. Now a certain man was there who had an infirmity thirty-eight years. When Jesus saw him lying there, and knew that he already had been* in that condition *a long time, He said to him, "Do you want to be made well?" The sick man answered Him, "Sir, I have no man to put me into the pool when the water is stirred up; but while I am coming, another steps down before me." Jesus said to him, "Rise, take up your bed and walk." And immediately the man was made well, took up his bed, and walked. And that day was the Sabbath.*

Mark 5:25–34

Now a certain woman had a flow of blood for twelve years, and had suffered many things from many physicians. She had spent all that she had and was no better, but rather grew worse. When she heard about Jesus, she came behind Him in the crowd and touched His garment. For she said, "If only I may touch His clothes, I shall be made well." Immediately the fountain of her blood was dried up, and she felt in her body that she was healed of the affliction. And Jesus, immediately knowing in Himself that power had gone out of Him, turned around in the crowd and said, "Who touched My clothes?" But His disciples said to Him, "You see the multitude thronging You, and You say, 'Who touched Me?'" And He looked around to see her who had done this thing. But the woman, fearing and trembling, knowing what had happened to her, came and fell down before Him and told Him the whole truth. And He said to her, "Daughter, your faith has made you well. Go in peace, and be healed of your affliction."

Mark 2:1–12

And again He entered Capernaum after some days, and it was heard that He was in the house. Immediately many gathered together, so that there was no longer room to receive them, not even near the door. And He preached the word to them. Then they came to Him, bringing a paralytic who was carried by four men. And when they could not come near Him because of the crowd, they uncovered the roof where He was. So when they had broken through, they let down the bed on which the paralytic was lying. When Jesus saw their faith, He said to the paralytic, "Son, your sins are forgiven you." And some of the scribes were sitting there and reasoning in their hearts, "Why does this Man speak blasphemies like this? Who can forgive sins but God alone?" But immediately, when Jesus perceived in His spirit that they reasoned thus within themselves, He said to them, "Why do you reason about these things in your hearts? Which is easier, to say to the paralytic, 'Your sins are forgiven you,' or to say, 'Arise, take up your bed and walk'? But that you may know that the Son of Man has power on earth to forgive sins"—He said to the paralytic, "I say to you, arise, take up your bed, and go to your house." Immediately he arose, took up the bed, and went out in the presence of them all, so that all were amazed and glorified God, saying, "We never saw anything like this!"

Mark 10:46–52

Now they came to Jericho. As He went out of Jericho with His disciples and a great multitude, blind Bartimaeus, the son of Timaeus, sat by the road begging. And when he heard that it was Jesus of Nazareth, he began to cry out and say, "Jesus, Son of David, have mercy on me!" Then many warned him to be quiet; but he cried out all the more, "Son of David, have mercy on me!" So Jesus stood still and commanded him to be called. Then they called the blind man, saying to him, "Be of good cheer. Rise, He is calling you." And throwing aside his garment, he rose and came to Jesus. So Jesus answered and said to him, "What do you want Me to do for you?" The blind man said to Him, "Rabboni, that I may receive my sight." Then Jesus said to him, "Go your way; your faith has made you well." And immediately he received his sight and followed Jesus on the road.

Mark 7:24–30

From there He arose and went to the region of Tyre and Sidon. And He entered a house and wanted no one to know it, but He could not be hidden. For a woman whose young daughter had an unclean spirit heard about Him, and she came and fell at His feet. The woman was a Greek, a Syro-Phoenician by birth, and she kept asking Him to cast the demon out of her daughter. But Jesus said to her, "Let the children be filled first, for it is not good to take the children's bread and throw it to the little dogs." And she answered and said to Him, "Yes, Lord, yet even the little dogs under the table eat from the children's crumbs." Then He said to her, "For this saying go your way; the demon has gone out of your daughter." And when she had come to her house, she found the demon gone out, and her daughter lying on the bed.

Matthew 20:25

But Jesus called them to Himself and said, "You know that the rulers of the Gentiles lord it over them, and those who are great exercise authority over them."

Philippians 3:13–14

Brethren, I do not count myself to have apprehended; but one thing I do, forgetting those things which are behind and reaching forward to those things which are ahead, I press toward the goal for the prize of the upward call of God in Christ Jesus.

Proverbs 23:7

For as he thinks in his heart, so is he. "Eat and drink!" he says to you, But his heart is not with you.

2 Corinthians 4:18

While we do not look at the things which are seen, but at the things which are not seen. For the things which are seen are temporary, but the things which are not seen are eternal.

Hebrews 12:1–2

Therefore we also, since we are surrounded by so great a cloud of witnesses, let us lay aside every weight, and the sin which so easily ensnares us, and let us run with endurance the race that is set before us, looking unto Jesus, the author and finisher of our faith, who for the joy that was set before Him endured the cross, despising the shame, and has sat down at the right hand of the throne of God.

Romans 10:13

For "whoever calls on the name of the Lord shall be saved."

Romans 13:14

But put on the Lord Jesus Christ, and make no provision for the flesh, to fulfill its lusts.

John 8:36

Therefore if the Son makes you free, you shall be free indeed.

Hebrews 6:12

That you do not become sluggish, but imitate those who through faith and patience inherit the promises.

2 Peter 1:3–4

As His divine power has given to us all things that pertain *to life and godliness, through the knowledge of Him who called us by glory and virtue, by which have been given to us exceedingly great and precious promises, that through these you may be partakers of the divine nature, having escaped the corruption* that is *in the world through lust.*

Colossians 1:13

He has delivered us from the power of darkness and conveyed us *into the kingdom of the Son of His love.*

Lesson 16
Healing Is a Harvest
Instructor
Barry Bennett

Note: All scriptures used in this lesson are quoted from the *New King James Version*.

I. We are born again by the incorruptible seed of God's Word, and in that truth, we find that God's Word is a seed. The seed that we hear—the seed that brings faith to our hearts—is the Word of God.

> *Having been born again, not of corruptible seed but incorruptible, through the word of God which lives and abides forever.*
>
> 1 Peter 1:23

   A. The incorruptible seed of God's Word carries the nature of God, His purpose, and it finds the soil of our hearts. When the seed of God's Word finds the soil of our hearts, depending upon the condition of the soil of our hearts, it will bring forth according to its nature. This is how the kingdom works.

II. Everything in the kingdom works according to the concept of the seed and of the law of seed, time, and harvest.

   A. The seed in the parable of the sower is the Word of God. Jesus taught about a man who sowed seed on the ground. The seed found different kinds of soil, different kinds of hearts. Some hearts may be flustered with the cares of this life and others may be soil of a good heart, a heart that's ready to receive.

> *Now the parable is this: The seed is the word of God.*
>
> Luke 8:11

   B. You can't see the fruit of God's Word until it brings forth its nature. These invisible Word seeds create visible life—creation and everything that we see.

By faith we understand that the worlds were framed by the word of God, so that the things which are seen were not made of things which are visible.

Hebrews 11:3

C. We live in a word-oriented, or a word-created, world that is sustained by the Word of God. And God's words are seeds that carry within them the nature and purpose of God.

D. God's Word is an expression of Himself, and He is constantly ready to bring forth what it contains, just like a seed. The Word of God is just waiting on the right environment: good soil, sun, and water. It's packaged and ready to go.

Then the LORD said to me, "You have seen well, for I am ready to perform My word."

Jeremiah 1:12

E. God's Word is being compared both to rain and to seed. The rain, or Word, that comes down from heaven is to give seed to the sower. There is provision for us. God's Word, like a seed, carries infinite abundance, potential, and prosperity in order to bring forth God's nature and purpose.

For as the rain comes down, and the snow from heaven, And do not return there, But water the earth, And make it bring forth and bud, That it may give seed to the sower And bread to the eater, So shall My word be that goes forth from My mouth; It shall not return to Me void, But it shall accomplish what I please, And it shall prosper in the thing for which I sent it.

Isaiah 55:10–11

III. Health and healing will be the harvests of what we have sown or what others have sown into us. The whole of creation is a function of God's Word and is sustained by God's Word, which is alive, active, and ready to be performed according to the concept of seed. All it is waiting for is a heart that believes.

A. A seed carries the nature of its source. A promise of God carries the nature of where it came from: the nature of God, the purpose of God, the vision of God, the prosperity of God, the abundance of God, the restoration of God, and the healing of God. It's all going to be contained in the seed of that promise.

B. A seed will reproduce according to its kind. Every promise of God, every Word of God, is going to reproduce according to its kind or according to its nature. If it is a promise about healing, it is going to reproduce according to what has been packaged inside: healing.

C. A seed carries infinite potential and is only limited by the kind of soil in which it is planted. A seed that finds a heart of unbelief is very limited in what it can produce. A seed, or a promise of God, that finds a heart that is prepared to believe will fully produce according to God's nature and purpose.

IV. Faith comes for healing in the same way it comes for salvation.

So then faith comes by hearing, and hearing by the word of God.
Romans 10:17

A. Faith is born in the soil of your heart by hearing the seed of God's Word. The condition of the heart will determine how well you hear. A heart that is hungry for God will hear God more clearly than a heart that doesn't care. Faith for salvation comes from hearing the message of salvation. The message of salvation, or the seed of the message, reproduces according to its kind.

But what does it say? "The word is near you, in your mouth and in your heart" (that is, the word of faith which we preach): that if you confess with your mouth the Lord Jesus and believe in your heart that God has raised Him from the dead, you will be saved. For with the heart one believes unto righteousness, and with the mouth confession is made unto salvation.
Romans 10:8–10

B. The same seed that got you saved gets you healed. The words used for faith and for salvation (Rom. 10:8–10), *sozo* and *soteria*, both include physical healing and forgiveness.

C. This is so powerful because we've limited salvation to simply the invisible forgiveness side of the issue. We haven't seen that it includes the physical, tangible part called healing.

D. When Jesus ministered, He went around forgiving sins and healing the sick. He was demonstrating the Gospel message, the invisible message of the kingdom, by delivering visible, tangible healing.

Who Himself bore our sins in His own body on the tree, that we, having died to sins, might live for righteousness—by whose stripes you were healed.

1 Peter 2:24

V.   Healing is a harvest.

A.   We're very quick to accept and understand that righteousness has been imputed to us and that righteousness is a gift. But healing has been imputed to you too; healing is also a gift.

Surely He has borne our griefs And carried our sorrows; Yet we esteemed Him stricken, Smitten by God, and afflicted. But He was wounded for our transgressions, He was bruised for our iniquities; The chastisement for our peace was upon Him, And by His stripes we are healed.

Isaiah 53:4–5

B.   Theologically, we've made healing something where maybe God will, or maybe God won't. That is a lie that we have to get out of our hearts and minds. We need to understand that the full package of God's redemptive work through Jesus on the cross is available, if your heart is willing to receive it.

C.   To cooperate with the seed of God's Word, we use the way we think, the way we speak, our actions, our feelings, and our emotions. We will cooperate either with God's Word or with the enemy.

D.   The seed of God's Word is available to you right now. The promises of God are all yes and amen, and they will produce according to their kind. They have no choice. The more fertile the soil of your heart, the more you will produce the nature of the promise, the nature of the seed of God's Word.

For all the promises of God in Him are Yes, and in Him Amen, to the glory of God through us.

2 Corinthians 1:20

E.   You will harvest what you cooperate with. If you're cooperating with a negative attitude, negative words, negative everything in your life, that is what you will harvest.

F. I am cooperating with God's seed that created all things, upholds all things, and carries His life and His nature. The Word of God is what I'm going to cooperate with, think about, speak about, and act on. I'm going to act like it's real. That's called faith.

Now faith is the substance of things hoped for, the evidence of things not seen.

Hebrews 11:1

G. Even if I believe in healing with my mind, if I never sow or allow any healing seeds to be sown into my life, I will never harvest that which has not been planted.

H. You may believe in your head that healing exists, that Jesus can heal, and that healing is your right and your benefit. You may believe it with your head, but you have to believe it with your heart. You can't create spiritual reality from your mind. It has to be from your heart; with the heart man believes.

I. As the seed of God comes into your heart, and you begin to speak and call it forth, you begin to stand on the promises with your mouth. This is cooperating with the Word of God, which bears the nature of God and the purpose of God for your life.

J. The kingdom of God is a seed kingdom. Our success in the kingdom of God is dependent upon how well we understand the concept of seed, time, and harvest.

K. The physical is a reflection of what is going on internally. Our attitudes, thought life, words, emotional stability, anxiety, depression, lack of peace, lack of joy, and everything that is going wrong in our lives are all harvests that have an impact upon the desire to be physically healed. All of these things are interrelated.

 1. What you feed your mind, what you allow your eyes to see, what you allow your ears to hear, and what you feed your body are seeds that will have a harvest.

VI. When we talk about health and healing, it's not just the subject of physical healing—it's about the whole being—spirit, soul, and body.

Beloved, I pray that you may prosper in all things and be in health, just as your soul prospers.

3 John 1:2

A. Every part of us needs to be prospering in the seeds of God's Word. We take time to sow the Word into our hearts, to think about the Word, to speak the Word, and to act upon the Word. If we get the whole being—spirit, soul and body—involved and cooperating with God's Word on every level, we will harvest health.

VII. Time is involved: the seed must sprout and grow. So many Christians wake up at some point in their life and ask, "I wonder how I got here?" It took time. It's the harvest of seeds sown into your life.

And He said, "The kingdom of God is as if a man should scatter seed on the ground, and should sleep by night and rise by day, and the seed should sprout and grow, he himself does not know how. For the earth yields crops by itself: first the blade, then the head, after that the full grain in the head. But when the grain ripens, immediately he puts in the sickle, because the harvest has come."

Mark 4:26–29

A. This is a chronology of events; things take place and we begin to see what we've sown.

B. If I'm dealing with sickness, anguish, depression, emotional distress, frustration, or otherwise, the first blade to sprout is an identifier of what I've been sowing. In my physical body, when I begin to notice something is out of whack, it is an identifier that I haven't been sowing correctly. There are some things that can be changed as I cooperate more with God in sowing health into my life on every level.

C. Health can be a genetic harvest. If there was something wrong genetically, sometimes that harvest is evident at birth. It doesn't mean God can't fix it. We have genetic weaknesses. Those are harvests from Adam's sin.

D. We have emotional issues. We may have been fed Twinkies® and Coca-Cola® for our whole life, so we harvest health issues from a poor diet. Whether it's genetic, emotional, mental, physical, or dietary, everything has a seed source. So, all of us are harvesting all the time from whatever has been sown into us.

E. Some harvests are immediate. If you say an ugly word to someone, you may get an immediate harvest. Some harvests are long term. It may take years to see the full result of certain seeds that have been sown into your life.

They became aware of it and fled to Lystra and Derbe, cities of Lycaonia, and to the surrounding region. And they were preaching the gospel there. And in Lystra a certain man without strength in his feet was sitting, a cripple from his mother's womb, who had never walked. This man heard Paul speaking. Paul, observing him intently and seeing that he had faith to be healed, said with a loud voice, "Stand up straight on your feet!" And he leaped and walked.

Acts 14:6–10

F.   Paul could perceive that the Word he was preaching created an expectation in the man's heart. It's still seed, time, and harvest. The only thing that's different is the time was compressed into just a matter of seconds, but he still heard the Word. It was evident to Paul and the command instigated a response: the man leaped up and walked.

G.   When the seed of God's Word finds the soil of a heart, belief is born, confession is made, and the miracle takes place. It's still seed, time, and harvest. So, whether the harvest of health and healing is immediate, or whether it's a process, don't stop sowing.

Therefore He who supplies the Spirit to you and works miracles among you, does He do it by the works of the law, or by the hearing of faith?

Galatians 3:5

VIII. Everything is Word related. People came to hear Jesus. They came to have the Word sown, and they came to harvest the result, the nature of the Word that was being sown—healing.

However, the report went around concerning Him all the more; and great multitudes came together to hear, and to be healed by Him of their infirmities.

Luke 5:15

A.   If we can completely cooperate with God on every level—spirit, soul, and body—the physical manifestation will come much easier.

B.   Your ears, your eyes, your heart, and your attitude are all seed gates. We're either opening our gates to the world, full of doubt and fear, or to the Word of God, full of faith and power.

For the hearts of this people have grown dull. Their ears are hard of hearing, And their eyes they have closed, Lest they should see with their eyes and hear with their ears, Lest they should understand with their hearts and turn, So that I should heal them.

Matthew 13:15

C. Let the Word of God be sown into you continually. Don't give up, don't become passive, and don't grow lazy. Keep the seed of God's Word in the midst of your heart.

My son, give attention to my words; Incline your ear to my sayings. Do not let them depart from your eyes; Keep them in the midst of your heart; For they are *life to those who find them, And health to all their flesh.*

Proverbs 4:20–22

LESSON REVIEW QUESTIONS

1. How do seed, time, and harvest work in a person's life?

2. According to Romans 10:17 and Luke 17:6, where does the seed of faith for healing come from, and how does it grow?

3. What is the incorruptible seed talked about in 1 Peter 1:23?

4. How do seed, time, and harvest apply to healing?

5. What role does God's Word have in bringing a harvest of healing?

6. Why do you think Christians aren't seeing a harvest of health in their lives?

**LESSON REVIEW
ANSWERS**

1. How do seed, time, and harvest work in a person's life?

   Everything, in both the natural and the supernatural, functions according to the law of seed, time, and harvest. Everything in our lives is a harvest of seeds sown by us or by others.

2. According to Romans 10:17 and Luke 17:6, where does the seed of faith for healing come from, and how does it grow?

   Faith comes for healing in the same way it comes for salvation—by hearing the Word of God. The seed of God's Word and His promises must be sown into our hearts. Then the seeds of faith must be spoken for faith to grow.

3. What is the incorruptible seed talked about in 1 Peter 1:23?

   The incorruptible seed is God's Word, and contained inside that seed is the very nature of God. This seed will reproduce according to the seed's nature. So, power, authority, and healing are in the nature of that seed.

4. How do seed, time, and harvest apply to healing?

   Possible answers: You're healed by the seeds you sow from the Word; some healings are immediate and some take time; you can't reap something that you didn't sow, but if you sow God's Word in faith, then you can reap healing; health and healing will be the harvest of God's Word that we have sown or others have sown into us.

5. What role does God's Word have in bringing a harvest of healing?

   Possible answer: God's Word carries God's nature, life, and authority for healing. The more you sow His Word into your life, the more you will see the harvest of healing in your body.

6. Why do you think Christians aren't seeing a harvest of health in their lives?

   Answers will vary.

POINTS TO PONDER

- A seed carries within it the potential for infinite increase and multiplication. All of that is packaged in the seed. The seed is programmed to reproduce according to its nature. The seed is the Word of God. We were born again by the incorruptible seed of God's Word, and everything that salvation implies was packaged in the seed of God's Word. It found the soil of your heart and you agreed, believed, and confessed with your mouth—this is how the kingdom works.

- Everything is based upon seed, time, and harvest, and every word from God is a seed that is looking for the good soil of your heart.

- The more Word you receive, the more you will produce wholeness in your life.

- If healing has been packaged into a promise, that's a seed that's looking for the good soil of your heart. It will reproduce according to its kind, and you should have an expectation based upon the nature of that promise, the nature of that seed.

- Salvation includes physical healing. It's the same seed. It carries the same nature of God. So, let's not divide and keep some of the blessing of salvation off on one side; it's all part of the same seed of God's Word.

- Your healing is closer than you may have thought. It's in the Gospel that you have believed and confessed with your mouth, but perhaps lack of knowledge has kept you from understanding that seed was there.

- The same redemptive work—that same all-inclusive, spirit, soul, and body redemption that took place on the cross—includes the provision for physical healing. We've got to understand that when we're hearing the Gospel, we're sowing a seed that contains everything we need—spirit, soul and body. Healing is a part of the package.

- We are either cooperating with the finished work of Christ, with the flesh, or with the devil. As we walk through life, we're either going to cooperate with the seed of God's Word, the finished work of Christ, or we're going to cooperate with our flesh and the symptoms.

- If you're not happy with the harvest, change the seed.

- We get to choose. We're sowing all the time in everything that we do. We sow by forgiving or not forgiving. We sow by walking in joy or in bitterness. We sow by being stingy or giving cheerfully. We sow by what we eat, whether that's garbage or good food. We sow with our attitudes and our expectations.

- Some harvests are a process and some harvests are immediate. Regardless, they still flow and function according to the principle of the seed. There is no difference; only the time element is different, even for miracles. Miracles are a result of seed, time, and harvest.

- Many times we're trying to get healing, but we're still unforgiving, bitter, cranky, mad, or whatever. So, we're trying to get healed without caring for the soil of our hearts.

- Don't wait on the manifestation; keep sowing. When you wait on the manifestation, you're waiting for your body to tell you whether you're healed or not. Let God's Word be the final word.

- Health is a harvest. Continually sow the Word of God into your heart. Don't let it depart from your eyes, from your ears, or from your heart. Keep it there because it will produce according to its nature. It will fulfill the purpose that God sent it to accomplish.

GO DEEPER

Self–Examination Questions

What seeds may have caused your harvest of physical problems?

Are you unhappy with harvest in some area of your life? What can you change?

What changes can you make in your life to sow more seeds toward a harvest of healing?

Prayer Points

Use these prayer points to write and pray your own powerful prayer:

- Thank God for the concept of seed, time, and harvest.
- Thank God for the power of His Word.
- Thank God for the power of the seed.
- Thank God that His Word brings forth harvest.
- Thank God that He purposes that we walk in health.
- Declare that you will change what you are sowing and what others are sowing into you.
- Commit to guard your heart and to continue sowing into it the Word of God.
- Commit to declare the Word of God over your health.
- Praise God that you will receive a harvest of healing and health.

Action Steps

- In your Healing University journal, illustrate how seed, time, and harvest work in your life and your healing. Make a visual representation and label the parts of the concept so you can remember how important it is to sow God's Word, get spiritual revelation, declare it, and then reap your harvest. You may want to draw your illustration or film a short video to put on social media. Find a way to convey these thoughts and share the revelation with others.

- Settle in your heart that everything in the kingdom of God and in life really works according to seed, time, and harvest—including health and healing. What you sow in your heart is important because that is what you will reap. Examine your heart and, when you are ready, make the following declaration and don't waver from it:

I believe that my healing depends on seed, time, and harvest. I will sow God's Word into my heart, declare His promises, and reap healing as my harvest.

_____ (sign and date)

- Read the following confession aloud and memorize it to internalize these promises and declarations of faith:

> By His stripes I am healed. Praise God. His Word is life and health to my flesh. His Spirit quickens my mortal body. Life and health is in the power of my tongue. I'm going to sow the seeds of life and health. The fruit of my righteousness is the Tree of Life. He sent His word and healed me. I bless the Lord with all that is within me. I bless the Lord and forget none of His benefits. He has forgiven all of my iniquities; He has healed all my diseases. He has redeemed my life from destruction and crowned me with loving kindness and tender mercy.

- Write your own answer to this question: _How will I see healing as a harvest in my life?_

DDITIONAL THOUGHTS

- There are foundational truths we must know in order to understand how seed, time, and harvest affect our health and our healing.

- God's Word is designed with potential, multiplication, and increase in mind. If it finds the right environment, it will produce; it will not return void.

- You can't change the past, but you can change the future, and you can change your future health. It might require a new kind of seed and a new determination to change how we look at our bodies, how we take care of ourselves, and what kind of Word we sow into ourselves.

- My physical health will be a function of what I've allowed myself to do: the exercise I do or don't do, the food I eat or don't eat, and the amount of sleep I get or don't get. All of those things are seeds that will have a harvest. Some harvests come very quickly; some harvests take years.

- The promise of God that will heal you is near you. Hopefully, it's in your mouth and coming from your heart.

- Your healing is a harvest of the words you choose to believe and allow into your heart. You choose those things to come out as a declaration.

- Just because you believe in healing doesn't mean you will reap healing. You're not healed by what you know; you're healed by what you sow.

- A sickness is only as powerful as your lack of revelation that you have authority over it.

- If you're not taking care of the soil of your heart, you're going to have weeds, and weeds will suck the life right out of you physically, mentally, and spiritually.

- A farmer harvests from the seed he has sown. You can't go harvest from somebody else's field. You harvest from what you have sown. You harvest from what you have watered, what you have fertilized, what you have cared for, what you have watched over, what you have protected, and what you are focused on. If you're not taking care of your seed, you will have weeds.

- Don't mix up the seed. Don't sow bad seed physically and try to sow good seed spiritually; get everything in line. Sow naturally good things into your body, sow good thoughts into your head, sow good words into your environment, sow the Word of God into your heart, and then speak it forth. You will see your health begin to conform to what God had in mind.

SCRIPTURES

Healing Is a Harvest

1 Peter 1:23

Having been born again, not of corruptible seed but incorruptible, through the word of God which lives and abides forever.

Luke 8:11

Now the parable is this: The seed is the word of God.

Hebrews 11:3

By faith we understand that the worlds were framed by the word of God, so that the things which are seen were not made of things which are visible.

Hebrews 1:3

Who being the brightness of His glory and the express image of His person, and upholding all things by the word of His power, when He had by Himself purged our sins, sat down at the right hand of the Majesty on high.

Jeremiah 1:12

Then the LORD said to me, "You have seen well, for I am ready to perform My word."

Isaiah 55:10–11

For as the rain comes down, and the snow from heaven, And do not return there, But water the earth, And make it bring forth and bud, That it may give seed to the sower And bread to the eater, So shall My word be that goes forth from My mouth; It shall not return to Me void, But it shall accomplish what I please, And it shall prosper in the thing for which I sent it.

Romans 10:17

So then faith comes by hearing, and hearing by the word of God.

Romans 10:8-10

> *But what does it say? "The word is near you, in your mouth and in your heart" (that is, the word of faith which we preach): that if you confess with your mouth the Lord Jesus and believe in your heart that God has raised Him from the dead, you will be saved. For with the heart one believes unto righteousness, and with the mouth confession is made unto salvation.*

1 Peter 2:24

> *Who Himself bore our sins in His own body on the tree, that we, having died to sins, might live for righteousness—by whose stripes you were healed.*

Isaiah 53:4-5

> *Surely He has borne our griefs And carried our sorrows; Yet we esteemed Him stricken, Smitten by God, and afflicted. But He was wounded for our transgressions, He was bruised for our iniquities; The chastisement for our peace was upon Him, And by His stripes we are healed.*

2 Corinthians 1:20

> *For all the promises of God in Him are Yes, and in Him Amen, to the glory of God through us.*

Hebrews 11:1

> *Now faith is the substance of things hoped for, the evidence of things not seen.*

Romans 12:2

> *And do not be conformed to this world, but be transformed by the renewing of your mind, that you may prove what is that good and acceptable and perfect will of God.*

3 John 1:2

> *Beloved, I pray that you may prosper in all things and be in health, just as your soul prospers.*

Mark 4:26-29

> *And He said, "The kingdom of God is as if a man should scatter seed on the ground, and should sleep by night and rise by day, and the seed should sprout and grow, he himself does not know how. For the earth yields crops by itself: first the blade, then the head, after that the full grain in the head. But when the grain ripens, immediately he puts in the sickle, because the harvest has come."*

Luke 17: 6

So the Lord said, "If you have faith as a mustard seed, you can say to this mulberry tree, 'Be pulled up by the roots and be planted in the sea,' and it would obey you."

Acts 14:6–10

They became aware of it and fled to Lystra and Derbe, cities of Lycaonia, and to the surrounding region. And they were preaching the gospel there. And in Lystra a certain man without strength in his feet was sitting, a cripple from his mother's womb, who had never walked. This man heard Paul speaking. Paul, observing him intently and seeing that he had faith to be healed, said with a loud voice, "Stand up straight on your feet!" And he leaped and walked.

Galatians 3:5

Therefore He who supplies the Spirit to you and works miracles among you, does He do it by the works of the law, or by the hearing of faith?

Luke 5:15

However, the report went around concerning Him all the more; and great multitudes came together to hear, and to be healed by Him of their infirmities.

Matthew 13:15

For the hearts of this people have grown dull. Their ears are hard of hearing, And their eyes they have closed, Lest they should see with their eyes and hear with their ears, Lest they should understand with their hearts and turn, So that I should heal them.

Proverbs 4:20–22

My son, give attention to my words; Incline your ear to my sayings. Do not let them depart from your eyes; Keep them in the midst of your heart; For they are life to those who find them, And health to all their flesh.

Many people have questions about healing and the following questions are ones which are typically asked. If you find that your questions aren't among these being answered, just remember that you can go to the Lord and ask the Holy Spirit to teach you (John 14:26) and guide you into truth (John 16:13). God loves your questions because He has the answers for your life, and your story is going to be a powerful testimony. Be encouraged to go back to the lessons and listen to them again. Review your notes and meditate on God's Word. Use these questions and answers, and the video teachings, to receive and walk in healing. Then start stepping out in boldness and pointing out the things of the enemy that he's trying to do in other people's lives.

1. Can bitterness and unforgiveness toward someone block my healing?

2. Is God willing to heal me even if my sickness is my fault?

3. Is all sickness related to what I eat?

4. Why do some people get healed the first time they get prayer?

About the Instructors

Andrew Wommack

Andrew Wommack's life was forever changed the moment he encountered the supernatural love of God on March 23, 1968. Since then, he has made it his mission to change the way the world sees God. The author of more than thirty books and the founder and president of Charis Bible College, Andrew brings the simplicity of the Word of God and the revelation of grace into every teaching. Throughout his years in ministry, Andrew has experienced an abundance of supernatural healings and miracles. With Andrew, students can expect to receive the truth of the Word from someone who has lived out all he teaches.

Carrie Pickett

Carrie Pickett has been a believer for over thirty years and has a passion for teaching God's Word. After graduating from Charis Bible College in 1999, she moved to Russia to plant a Charis campus. While in Russia, Carrie met her husband, Mike. Together they grew the Russian ministry to reach over ten Russian-speaking nations. After sixteen years in Russia, Carrie and Mike relocated to Colorado, where she now serves as the assistant vice president of Charis Bible College and director of the Global Training School. She has a heart to reach the world with the grace message and to see powerful ministers raised up.

Barry Bennett

Barry Bennett, a graduate of Christ for the Nations Institute in Dallas, Texas, has served the Lord since 1972. He and his wife, Betty Kay, have ministered in Mexico, Guatemala, and in Chile, where they spent almost twelve years before returning to Texas in 2001. Barry came to Andrew Wommack Ministries in 2007 and worked in the Phone Center as a prayer minister before accepting a position answering scriptural and doctrinal questions. Today, Barry serves as the dean of instructors and as an instructor at Charis Bible College Woodland Park. Barry is passionate about teaching the practical truths of God's Word.

Carlie Terradez

Carlie Terradez is an international speaker, author, and Charis Bible College adjunct instructor. She moved to the U.S. from the UK after graduating from Charis Bible College Walsall in 2008 with her husband, Ashley. Shortly after, Carlie and her husband were ordained by Andrew Wommack Ministries, which spurred the launch of Terradez Ministries. Carlie's life is a testimony to the miraculous power of God. Having received deliverance from numerous life-threatening conditions and seen her terminally ill daughter supernaturally healed, Carlie is passionate about helping others receive and walk in the abundant life that Jesus has provided.

Daniel Amstutz

Daniel Amstutz is the dean of worship arts and the director of Healing School at Charis Bible College Woodland Park. He is a seasoned, ordained minister and a published songwriter and recording artist. His lifelong passion is for the arts to be used for the glory of God. Daniel holds a bachelor of music from the University of Colorado and a bachelor of theology from Christian Life School of Theology. Daniel teaches several classes at Charis, including Prayer Minister Training, New Covenant Worship, and Lifestyle of Worship.

Greg Mohr

Greg Mohr is the director of Charis Bible College Woodland Park. He is a conference speaker and the author of several books, including *A Prosperous Soul,* and *Your Healing Door.* Greg has personal healing testimonies and is known for being an instructor who shares from his heart. Previously, Greg served as Senior Pastor of River of Life Church in Decatur, Texas, for twenty-four years. He is a graduate of Rhema Bible Training Center in Broken Arrow, Oklahoma, and has earned a master's degree in leadership from Southwestern Christian University in Bethany, Oklahoma. As an instructor at Charis, Greg teaches several classes and directs the third-year Ministry School.

Duane Sheriff

Duane Sheriff is the senior pastor of Victory Life Church in Durant, Oklahoma. He is gifted with an anointing to communicate the simplicity of the Gospel. He believes a personal and intimate relationship with the Lord is essential for every believer. God has given Pastor Duane an abundance of divine revelation, which pours forth as he shares and ministers the Word. His personal presentation of the Gospel resurrects hope and ignites faith. Duane is a frequent speaker at Charis Healing School and personally experienced the power of God with his grandson's miraculous healing in 2018.